Normal People's Problems

God bless,

Alton

Alton Fry Jr.

LifeRich Publishing is a registered trademark of
The Reader's Digest Association, Inc.

LifeRich Publishing books may be ordered through booksellers or by contacting:

LifeRich Publishing
1663 Liberty Drive
Bloomington, IN 47403
www.liferichpublishing.com
1 (888) 238-8637

ISBN: 978-1-4897-1949-2 (sc)
ISBN: 978-1-4897-1947-8 (hc)
ISBN: 978-1-4897-1948-5 (e)

Library of Congress Control Number: 2018958149

Print information available on the last page.

LifeRich Publishing rev. date: 11/16/2018

This book is dedicated to all the parents who have children who suffer from the addiction of meth. Thank you for loving us even when we didn't love ourselves.

I'm pumping gas when I notice the family on the other side of the pumps. They have two kids in the back seat, smiling and happy. I have two pounds of meth in my back seat, and I can't remember the last time I was smiling and happy. The husband is talking to his wife through the window about whether to get the kids chicken nuggets from McDonald's or Wendy's. I haven't eaten in three days. They'll go home tonight and sleep well in their cozy home, safe from the wilds of the world. I stand a very real chance of being robbed and murdered before the sun comes up. One of these days I'm gonna have me some Normal People's Problems.

I pray.

Everyday.

Sometimes a short prayer. Sometimes a long prayer.

But everyday it's the same prayer.

"God, just let my heart explode, just let my brain explode." "Just let me die."

"Die."

Take me away from this man-made hellhole. Stop this pain in my heart being caused by her absence. Take away this guilt that haunts my mind from the pain I have caused my family.

God, are you listening to me?

Just where are you?

I'm sitting here at Colwell probation detention in Blairsville, GA in what feels like my life's, my darkest hour, on the top tier of a three bed bunk bed, issued for free by the good state of Georgia. Staring out a small, dirt stained window, when, at four p.m. the sky goes completely dark.

I don't mean it got cloudy outside. I mean it went pitch black.

You see, today is the day of the 2017 eclipse and it just went black as midnight at four in the afternoon.

And then God answered me.

Believe what you want, but in my mind I heard God say "wait". It was the same soft, gentle voice, yet deep with emotion and love, that I had come to believe was my prayers being answered. I paused for a moment, and then asked, "OK God, what do you want me to wait for?"

After a few moments of deafening silence, I again heard my soul's creator speaking to my mind with the same single word that had troubled me all through out my impatient life.

"Wait."

After a few moments of no further celestial advise beyond his one word parables, I decided to retry and further our conversation. "I heard you the first time God, but I still don't know what it is you want me to wait on," I said in a tone not very becoming of someone who is speaking to God himself.

And, just like my first attempt at gaining information, I was once again shot down with a resounding nothing.

My soul, screaming for help, for comfort. My mind, praying for what I can only imagine as the cold comfort of death. My heart, feeling as if it had been attacked by a grizzly bear and ripped to shreds.

What do I get? "Wait."

And so, I sat silently, with no further response forth coming, just staring out of my window at another wonderful, beautiful, exciting thing in life I was missing due to my love affair with meth; when suddenly, just as quickly as it went completely dark at four in the afternoon, the sun light began to return as this weird mating of the sun and moon began to break.

And once again, I heard God speak. Only this time His words to me were very clear.

"Hey Fry, if you would just shut up and give me a minute my plan for you will be right before your eyes. You see, I created this eclipse. I turned the brightest hour of this day into it's darkest." "Kinda sounds like your life doesn't it?", the gentle voice continued. "You thought you were the king of your castle."

"You quit listening to me. You quite praying to me. You wouldn't even talk to me anymore, just as we're doing right now, the way two old friends should talk, the way a father and child who love each other should talk."

"Oh no, you had to go out on your own, be your own boss. I tried to get you to listen to me, to follow me once again, but you just turned your back because you thought you didn't need your old pal God anymore, you had life by the horns. And so here you are, locked up in a gangster day care. Don't blame me. Don't blame your family and don't blame her. BLAME YOURSELF."

"Yes, this may be your darkest hour, but look, my child and behold the power of your God. Just as quickly as I turned the day into night I have once again turned the darkness into light. So remember my child, THIS TOO SHALL PASS!"

"Just as I promised you, I will hold you through your darkest hour and won't let go. Believe in your heavenly Father and the plan I have for you. I got you, Fry."

"Now, you got six months of just setting here, doing nothing, so go do something with your time and start writing that book that you and "her" have talked about for years."

Oh, and by the way, "her" is the most beautiful, crazy, ride or die woman to walk this planet. My purdygurl. My Devon. My partner in crime, my wife, my ex-wife, my best friend.

In short, my world.

So welcome to normal people's problems. The true life adventures of a meth'ed up Bonnie and Clyde.

I'm sure you will laugh a little, cry a little, more than likely get confused at some of the things I write and want to scream at the top of your lungs, "why did you do that, you big dummy?" One simple answer that's not so simple.

DRUGS!

They make you do things a normal person would never think of doing. You begin to have thoughts that would never cross a sane person's mind.

Which brings me to my point. What you are about to read is the true telling of our lives. I didn't make any of this up. I'm sure I may have added a word or two here and there just to add a little flavor, but every story is true. I will, however, be leaving out a few memories of mine and Devon's that are ours and ours alone

Many things have been taken from us, and so I ask your forgiveness for not sharing these few precious moments with you. We have lead a life of daring passion and impulsive excitement. You will find out more about us than you probably really wanted to know, but I have a few wonderful memories that will remain in my heart and dreams, forever to be mine and only mine. I love you Devon. Forever, plus a day.

chapter 2

Love At First Sight

Now, it may seem a bit strange to you for me to start this story in 1998, simply ignoring the first 28 years of my life. But the truth is, I don't think I ever felt alive until the day I met Devon. I guess the only thing I'm proud of out of my first 28 is my daughter, Taylor. She is a true Georgia peach. Smart beyond smart and the looks to go with it. Independent in a way that would make any parent proud. I use the term parent loosely. Half her DNA may be mine, but in no way can I take any credit for the incredible woman she has turned out to be. Well, maybe a little, if, and only if, you count setting bad examples on how not to live your life. Thank you God for giving her the brains to learn from my mistakes.

But I digress. Back to our story. Let me start by saying this, my parents didn't raise a drug addict. They didn't raise a drug dealer. They raised me to be a good and honorable man. I turned myself into what I had become. No one but me. I just wanted to make that perfectly clear.

Now on with our story.

A lot of things had to fall into place for me and Devon to have ever met. The year was 1998 and mine and Daddy's masonry business was booming. We were bricking a house for this lady who had moved to Clarkesville from West Virginia. About half way through the job her cousin Jake, this hillbilly kid from the same coal mine town she was from showed up on her doorstep for a visit. He decides he likes Clarkesville and asked her if he can stay awhile. She says sure as long as you get a job. They show up on the site of her new home, we get to talking, and, as they say, the rest is history.

It didn't take Jake but about a week of living in Clarkesville to find out we had a community college, that, to a young man like himself, is fertile hunting ground for the opposite sex. He meets a young lady named Lisa, from Atlanta, who is going to school in Clarkesville and they quickly fall in love. After meeting the man of her dreams, Lisa thinks it is time to invite her best friend, who lives in Newton, Ga about one hour south of Atlanta, up to Clarkesville for the weekend to meet her prince charming.

OK, let's recap.

We have the local yokel, me, who has lived in Clarkesville his whole life, who meets the hillbilly kid from West Virginia that has been in Clarkesville for one week, that, in turn, meets a girl that lives two hours away, but has decided her life's outlook would be much rosier by going to school in Clarkesville, who in turn invites her best friend, who lives three hours away to come and visit her in Clarkesville for the weekend.

Sounds about right.

It was Friday afternoon when I got the call from Jake asking me to bring him a small sack of dope. Well, this immediately sent up a red flag, because he had just left my house two hours earlier with quite a large sack of meth for himself.

I asked him what was going on and he replied that his girlfriend, Lisa, had invited her best friend up for the weekend to see where she was going to school, and, of course to also meet her new boyfriend, Jake. After getting together with a few other people that she was going to school with, they decided to kick their get together up a notch with some meth.

Jake explained to me that although he had plenty of dope left in his sack, he just didn't feel "comfortable" dealing with any of these people that he knew nothing about, except for his girlfriend's marijuana laced declaration that "their all cool", a vouch, that apparently had no backbone with him.

"Ok, Jake, let me get this straight," I began. "You're out partying with people that you don't trust enough to sell dope to, so you think it's a good idea to call me and ask me to come sell to the same people?"

"Yeah, bro, do you mind?"

"That must be some really good pot yaw smoking cuz it's done got you plain stupid," I said, trying to remain calm.

"Yeah, bro, it is some good pot," he mumbled. "So you comin' to see us or what, bro?" He continued.

"First off, stop calling me bro. you know I hate pot and the way it makes people act and talk," which, as a side note is very true. I didn't smoke pot nor did I even like being around people who did. I was a meth addict. PERIOD. I wasn't one of those people who did whatever kind of drug was in from of them.

"Second off," I continued, "does it make the least bit of sense to you that if you're too worried to deal with these people, why would I want to deal with them?"

"Because they gots plenty of money."

"Where did you say you were?" As the businessman in me threw all common sense out the window, which was a major issue with me. Stick enough money in my face and you and I would become long lost best friends. It's true that I was an addict, but meth wasn't my only addiction. The money was just as powerful, if not more, than the meth. It was absolutely amazing the doors meth would open up, but even more astounding, in some cases, the people who would provide the money for the meth to keep those doors open.

And that's all that will be said about that.

Thirty minutes later, I'm pulling up to Joe's house, a mutual friend of mine and Jake's, who was his pot dealer, and also just happened to be the spot where Jake and his new friends decided to gather and party for the night.

I walk in, find Joe, and ask him if we can speak privately in the back. We go to his bedroom to discuss the situation, and much to my dismay, I find out that beyond Jake and his girlfriend, Lisa, he doesn't know any of the four other people gathered in his living room either. Seeing as how he's already sold them pot does little to calm my fears of a possible set up, and does little to take me off edge.

I walk back into the living room where all these stoners are sitting, look at this beautiful blonde that I have never seen before, and say, "Hey you, let me see your drivers license."

"What are you going to do, I.D. me to buy drugs?" was her response as she handed over her drivers license.

"No," I replied, while at the same time pulling my pistol out of my waist band and laying it down beside me, "but let me make this clear, Miss Devon Sanderlin of Newnan, GA, I promise you that if I get pulled over leaving here and get arrested, when I bond out, and I will bond out, I'm gonna come down to your house and tie your parents up and make you watch as I burn their house down around them."

"You feel me?"

"Yes, I believe I do" she spoke with a changed attitude.

Needless to say, the guy sitting next to her, another one in the group of folks I didn't know, had his drivers license out and ready before I even looked his way.

I'm one of those people who's bark is much worse than his bite, but they didn't know that. I took care of business, and thank goodness, had a successful exit.

I went about the rest of my night and never had another thought about Jake and his new friends until...

chapter 3

The Story of Goldilocks

I had plans for the evening so I told Jake that he could borrow my house for a couple of hours to hang out with his girlfriend. At this point in my life I was living dangerously foolish or foolishly dangerous. I guess it just depended on who you were asking.

I had just came out of a divorce and was broken-hearted. I didn't care much about anything or anyone, especially myself, and the amount of meth I was doing showed such. For whatever reasons, my night didn't go as planned, which, in the life of a meth dealer, is to be expected. So, I decided to just cut my losses and call it a night and head back home.

It was around 1 a.m. when I got there and much to my surprise, Jake's girlfriend's car was still sitting in my driveway. I got out of my truck and walked quietly to my front door, which, you'll find out is house rule number one of mine; day or night. You come to my house you had better be quiet. Anyways, I walked in to my humble abode, and low and behold, there sets none other than Miss Devon Sanderlin of Newnan, GA. The little smart mouth, yet beautiful, chick who just a few hours earlier I was "I.D.ing" to buy meth, at gun point.

Oh yeah, let's not forget the death threats to her parents.

I don't know whether I was more surprised and confused at her being there in my home, or if she was more concerned and scared about why this gun toting, redneck meth dealer just walked into the house that she was told belonged to her best friends' boyfriend, Jake. In her zeal to try and impress Devon, Jake's girlfriend had told her that it was Jake's house. The nice car sitting in the yard was also Jake's. In fact, they just told her my whole life story as if it were his, never thinking that I would be coming home that night to find her sitting on my couch.

Well, after about fifteen minutes of speaking with each other, I had finally assured her that she was, in fact, safe and that the house was actually mine.

I think pointing out all of the family photos of myself and my family hanging on the walls was what finally won her over.

We spent the night together in my living room. We talked about ourselves, our families, and the two friends we now had in common.

We laughed.

We kissed.

We talked a little more.

We kissed a lot more.

We quit talking.

To quote the great Oscar Wilde, "I like people better than I do principles, and I like people with no principles better than anything else in the world." I think that night, two Wilde fans met and fell in love.

I had been missing something in my life, what, I didn't really know. Or, at least I didn't want to admit. Maybe I loved the darkness so much because it held back the reality that came with the first rays of the sun. The shadows were my friends. I wasn't looking for realness. I wasn't looking for love. If anything I was just trying to find that piece of me that life had so cruelly stolen from me. Of course I didn't know it at the time, but this cute little yellow haired girl with the deep blue eyes would become that piece of me that I had been looking and longing for in my life. Nor did I realize at the time that this was the beginning of our descent into meth madness; looking for the greatest pleasures life had to offer.

I remember standing at my front door the next morning, watching the sun break over Alec mountain, thinking that something seemed different. Something. I looked over at my couch and saw what looked like a beauty out of one of the fairy tales that my father told to me as a child.

Her long blonde hair a mess; she was covered up with a blanket, revealing only her perfect face, full of slumber, wearing a slight smile that I would like to think was the result of our night together. She looked like an angel as the first rays of light began to filter through the window that was above my couch. I walked over, bent down, and gently kissed her lips that were already warm from the early morning sun.

I left her a note; I really hope you decide to visit again," and I walked out the door and into a new day. I don't know if this is true or not, but Devon likes to tell people that before she left to go home that morning, she told Lisa, her best friend, that she was going to marry me. Like I said, I don't know if she really said that or just tells me that. Either way, it doesn't matter because I know this to be truthful, I WAS IN LOVE WITH HER.

chapter 4

Now and Then

I hope you don't mind if I steer away from our story for a moment and give you an update on my current "situation".

I have been here at Carlton H. Colwell Probation Detention Center for almost two months now. With my time at White County jail included, I haven't seen home in the last six months.

Last night, I was lying in bed talking to God, which has become my usual routine now that I find myself locked in a world I know nothing about, and the first words out of my mouth were "hey God, I'm real proud of you".

"Oh yeah, Fry, and just what have I done to make you proud of me?" was the response I got from the gentle and loving voice that I have come to associate with God.

"Well, I'll tell you ole buddy," I began, "You have really been on the ball answering my prayers lately I been praying to you going on thirty five years now and I can't remember a time in all those years that you've done a better job AND been on time in answering my requests. I just thought I should let you know, good job God."

"Well Alton", I knew right then and there that I was going to get a talking to for the simple reason that he was no longer referring to me as Fry, but was now going all formal on me, calling me Alton.

"Well Alton, as much as I appreciate the compliment and the pat on the back, because God knows, oh wait, because I know I deserve a few kudos every once in a while, and it is nice to hear you give a prayer of just thanks, and don't get me wrong here, Fry, but, "whew, he went back to calling me Fry", once again you got it all wrong." he continued. "I have answered your prayers, both big ones and small ones, since the day you asked Me to come into your life when you were just a little boy. As far as that goes, I was answering prayers on your behalf before there was a you. You've been loved for a very long time, but it is only now that you are finally learning to accept my blessings for what they are. You see, you have just always told me what you need to happen in your life and then just expected me to jump right on it and make it happen. You never truly gave yourself to me or the plan I have for your life. I need all of you, your mind, heart, soul and body to believe, yet you always had a back up plan just in case I didn't answer your plans the way you saw fit. You never asked for MY WILL to be done in your life. It was always, "OK God, I'm telling you what I need for you to do for me, but just in case you're taking the day off or don't act as quickly as I THINK you should, I'm gonna keep my plan B on standby."

"Yeah, I guess your right," I answered, feeling like a school boy who had just got a paddling from his favorite teacher.

"There's been plenty of times that you have promised me that if I'll do this or that you will, in return, STOP doing this or that, but as we both know, Alton," oh no, he's back to Alton again, "As we both know Alton, your words were empty and your promises turned into lies. And to be quite honest with you, I had become tired of listening to your talk, talk, talk and was ready to see some action. What was it you were always telling Devon? Actions speak louder than words, correct?"

"Yes God, You are correct." I was sounding more defeated by the minute.

"And so, my child, that is why you are here today. You were on your way to dying. You were doing one of the finest jobs of killing yourself slowly that I have ever seen someone do and it hurt me. It made me weep to see what you were doing to yourself. It made me angry to see what you were doing to your mother and father and the pain and absolute agony you were causing them. Instead of giving you a shameful death that would have done nothing more than to inflict further suffering on people who didn't deserve it, I chose to give you another chance to prove yourself to me."

It was at this point that I know the exact reason that I thought God had started answering my prayers, or as he put it, I finally started seeing just how blessed I truly am, and for the first time in my life, I had opened my heart and eyes, to see that God had been answering my prayers all along.

I'll be the first to admit that things have come easy to me in life. My parents instilled in me the value of hard work and the value of a dollar. I made a lot of money in the masonry business and owning a video store. I also owned a game room that was quite profitable, and I'm not proud of this fact, but also a lot of cash in the dope game.

I'll also tell you that I have had many vices in my life. Truth be told, I am a man who has spent his life worshiping his senses.

I loved women, I loved gambling and I loved drugs and the power and money that came with it. I will never be one who wishes for immortality. People only wish to live forever because they choose not to enjoy life and feel that they have missed something or another along the way and with just a little more time will fill that void that eats away at them. The only thing missing in life is Devon.

Anyways, back to my point about my blessings. Every time I went to jail, either my parents or Devon was there to bond me out.

It came easy. I would go to court, say the words the judge wanted to hear and leave on probation. It came easy.

Let me give you a prime example of just how easy, or as I see more clearly now, just how blessed I was, and in fact, still am.

On July 3, 1999, the drug task force showed up at our front door. We were arrested for possession of marijuana, possession of meth, and possession of meth with intent to distribute. As we were sitting in the back of the cop car, handcuffed and heading to jail, I looked at Devon and said, "baby, if you'll keep your mouth shut and let me handle this, I will marry you, ok?"

"Ok baby," was her quick response.

Habersham County set our bonds at $40,000 each. My parents had us out in three days. Once again, easy. They kept putting our cases off until a year had passed with no end in sight, so Devon did the only thing a bride-to-be would do. She set our wedding date. She picked October 8th of 2000. Again, easy. After setting the date, she then booked us a cruise for our honeymoon for the following week, Easy. Also during this time, Devon decided that she wanted to go to college and get a degree. Why not? Sounds easy enough. Life was really going our way and then one day reality showed up and reared its ugly self and smacked us right up side the head.

I came home from work and walked in to find Devon setting in the living room floor, crying her eyes out. Before I could even say anything she threw a piece of paper at me that landed at my feet. Without even picking it up, I knew from the pain that was shooting through my heart exactly what it was.

We finally had a court date. It was scheduled for the Friday after our wedding, two days before we were to leave on our honeymoon cruise to the Bahamas. To make a long story short, the day of our trial, I took the two felonies we were charged with which allowed Devon to plead to a misdemeanor pot possession so she wouldn't lose her scholarship by being a felon. I was strapped with an ankle monitor two hours after court, meaning I could not go any further than twenty feet from my front door without it sending an alarm to my probation officer.

The rules were this; Monday through Friday I was allowed to go to work. I couldn't leave until 7:00 am and had to be home by 5:30 pm. If I were anywhere else besides work between those hours, I was going to jail. If I was caught out after curfew anywhere other than on my way to seeking medical attention for myself, I was going to jail. On Saturdays I was not allowed to leave, PERIOD. On Sundays my curfew was 10:30 am till 1:00 pm. Just to church and then a quick lunch at mom and dads', that is, as long as the preacher didn't get to long-winded. Other than that, I was told in no uncertain terms, that if the monitor said I was more than twenty feet away from its base, I could expect a visit from someone with handcuffs.

I was under house arrest.

Devon was beside herself. We had a beautiful wedding and now all her planning for our honeymoon was going to be for nothing. I couldn't let that happen. After all, I am her warrior, sworn to protect and defend her to the end. It was my job to make things right. And so, I pulled out my most lethal and dangerous weapon in my arsenal. My big mouth.

By the end of the day I had convinced the judge, my state probation officer and the private company that monitored my whereabouts to actually allow me to LEAVE THE COUNTRY to go on our cruise. I could not, however, talk them into waiting until our return to put the ankle monitor on me. They insisted that it had to be done right then and there, before I left their offices that day.

Compromise, Fry, compromise.

And so, as they're fitting me for my newest fashion accessory, they begin to explain the proper caring procedures for their device. If I cut it off = $2000. If I beat it or smash it = $2000. Any damage to the base, you guessed it, $2000. But the most important detail they wanted me to know before we left for our great water adventure was to not get the ankle monitor wet.

"I'm sorry, what was that you just said?"

'Get it wet and short out the internal electronics and it will cost you $2000." "OK, smart guy, tell me this, if you can't get it wet, then how am I supposed to take a shower with it on?"

"Take a bath with your ankle propped out of the water unless you want to pay us $2000, smart guy!"

We had no choice. We left and went home and started packing for our honeymoon, only we packed an extra bag. Thank God this was before 9-11, because I think we would have had a pretty hard time explaining why we were carrying a duffel bag full of gallon freezer bags and duct tape. Devon's Mom came up with the brilliant idea to wrap my foot and ankle with two gallon freezer bags and then duct tape the top to ensure that the electronics I was sporting didn't get wet. You think I'm lying? Well, as the old saying goes; been there done that, AND I have the pictures to prove it.

Like I was saying, our life was easy.

I got to marry the most beautiful woman I had ever seen. I didn't go to prison. Devon got to stay in school, and we got to go on our cruise.

Easy peasy.

All this, I thought, was due to my hard work, not God blessing us. I see now that he was answering prayers that weren't even being prayed. We were blessed. So blessed I now realize that we were drinking from the saucer because our cup had overflowed.

Looking back, I also realize that we took our love for granted as much as we did the sun being in the sky. It was an absolute of life. Something that never needed questioning. It was as if there had been no life before us. We were that great. But once again, sixteen years later, reality showed back up and this time knocked my head completely off my shoulders.

chapter 5

Not So Easy

Welcome to White County Detention Center. Once again, I thought "easy." I'll see my probation officer, say a few words of regret, maybe shed a tear, and I'll be home in a couple of days.

"HA." Again, I say "HA". Not this time ole boy. After ten days my probation officer still hadn't come to see me. After thirty days without so much as a peep, I was starting to lose my mind. Day thirty eight, this young lady with chubby cheeks and a cute smile showed up and introduced herself as my new probation officer and began to explain to me that due to the seriousness of my charges they were seeking a revocation hearing. That meant, if I lost, twenty years in prison.

At that point I was fresh out of charming words that had served me so well in the past and the tears that were now rolling down my face were very real.

And so I began to pray. Just like all the other times in my life when trouble had come my way, I started telling God what I needed him to do and I needed it done right now. And just like every other time in my life, I also started putting my back-up plan into place. You know, just in case God wasn't listening or was busy with someone a little more important and more worthy than myself.

I began to dwell on the fact that a twenty year prison sentence for a forty seven year old man might as well be the death sentence. I would get out to nothing. My Mom and Dad would both have passed on. My home would have been sold or foreclosed on, long before I would have been able to get out. What would I do with the rest of my life? What kind of job opportunities are there available for a sixty seven year old, new released convict?

NOTHING. ABSOLUTELY NOTHING.

Even if by some miracle I was able to find a job, how would I even get there?

But most of all, it was the thought of losing all the ones that I loved that kept my plan B alive. It drove me mad with rage to think about losing my parents while being behind bars. Never having Sunday lunch again. No more evenings on their front porch, just enjoying our rocking chairs. But most of all, the one single thing that helped me to make up my mind to implement plan B was the hunger. The gnawing at my soul. The one thing I knew I couldn't live without, Devon.

Just the thought of never being able to hold hands with her, to never again be able to feel her arms around me in a loving embrace. Never being able to feel the warmth of her breath on my shoulder as we make love.

NOPE. NOT GONNA HAPPEN.

And so I began the ground work for my plan B. I was going to kill myself. I started to collect some pretty heavy medications from one of the guys in my dorm who had some serious mental issues. He was trading me his sleeping pills and his anti-psychotic meds for food. Every night I would pray to God to deliver me home and every day I would collect a few more pills.

I couldn't face what the future had planned for me. I was sick and tired of being sick and tired. I was tired of letting my family down. Tired of letting myself down. Tired of letting God down.

I missed Devon and everyday my hunger for her presence grew stronger and stronger.

I looked around and realized that I was standing in the graveyard of my life. It all became too much. I saw no hope for the future and then I asked myself, "Is it better to die than to live without love and happiness?"

I began to pray harder than I had ever prayed before in my life, begging God to let me go home. Thinking about losing my parents while in prison, I found myself on my knees praying even harder for comfort. Thinking about a life without Devon, my prayers became constant. My prayers eventually turned into silent screams, trapped in my throat, like an emotional dam that held back my very life force. Those screams eventually turned into tears. My tears molded themselves into a ball of rage.

I found myself one night, in my private shower stall, kicking and punching the wall with a wash cloth in my mouth. I didn't want the people in the day room to hear my now real screams aimed at God and His unwillingness to answer my prayers.

And yet, every day I was still collecting pills, never fully trusting that God would answer my prayers. Always thinking that I knew better than God. I knew what was best for me and if He would just start doing His job, we would all be a lot better off.

But He refused to do what I told Him. He wasn't answering my prayers. I wasn't going home, so I continued on with my own plans. I sat down and wrote three letters.

My goodbye letters.

The first one was to my parents. It told them just how much I loved them and what an awesome job they had done raising me. I told my Mom she was the reason I had lived this long. She was my guiding light when my way grew dark. She was never short on hugs and kisses and I love yous for me. I told my Dad that he was my hero. Everything a man should be. All the things I would never be. He taught me how to hunt, fish and work. If I was half the man he was, I would still have my daughter calling me Daddy.

My next letter was to my very dear friend Wanda. She was my friend whether I had drugs or not. I love Wanda like a sister. She would sit and listen to me complain about Devon and then cry about how much I love her. She has seen the good, the bad, and the ugly in my life, and chose to never judge me. She is the kind of friend very few people have, but everyone needs. I asked her to remind our friends of the good things I did in life. I tried to be kind. To give help when needed. I tried to balance my bad deeds with as much good deeds as possible.

And my final letter was, of course, to Devon. It was the shortest letter of all. It simply read.

Our love broke my heart.

I was now ready to die. Every morning when I woke up, I asked myself, "is today the day? Will today be the day that my wallowing in "what ifs,' and "if I could onlys", finally end?"

Suicide works in one of two ways. A person has to have either a tremendous amount of courage to end their life, or, said person has to be afflicted with such despair that hope seems impossible. The courage, I was probably lacking. The despair, my tank was full. I had found the truth in myself and knew, beyond the shadow of a doubt, that my way out was the only way out. I could not face the painful boredom of wasting away for twenty years.

And then I heard God cry.

I had thirty five pills. More than enough to ease my tormented soul into rest. BUT I HEARD GOD WEEPING LIKE A CHILD. His tears were for me, or rather, because of me.

"My child, please listen to me," his voice still beautiful and gentle, but now full of pain. Pain that I was causing.

"Alton, abandon this foolish plan of yours and give your troubles to Me. Stop believing in yourself and trust Me when I tell you, I GOT THIS."

"God, I'm scared too. What if you don't do what I want you to do?"

"I have had you throughout your life. Even when you didn't know you needed Me, I was there. Give your faith to me. Truly trust in your God and once again I will see you through. Stop praying to Me to change your life the way you see fit. Instead, let go and let Me show you what your God can do for you."

I let go.

chapter 6

Olam Habah

It was 2:30 am. I got up out of my bed, walked over to the toilet and flushed all the pills I had been saving. Every single one.

"God," I began. "Life is stronger than me. The drugs are stronger than me. The last year has destroyed the man in me."

"Yes son, I know, your pain is also my pain. I know you have felt alone, but that's only because you choose to ignore me through the most difficult time of your life. Tonight was not the first time I have wept for you, Alton. Tonight was just the first time you chose to hear my sorrow over you. Do you know why?"

"No God, tell me."

"Because for the first time in a very long time, you have given yourself to me. You got out of your own way and decided to follow instead of lead. Do you remember Devon's favorite Bible verse?"

"Yes, I think I do. Faith without works is undone, right?"

"That's the very one. Well, tonight you showed me that your faith in Me is more than just talk. You gave Me your works. You showed Me that you're finally ready to let me do some of the heavy lifting for you. Your vow to Me will not be forgotten and in return I will show you the meaning of kindness and forgiveness.

23

"That was the devil you flushed down the toilet tonight. That was your lack of faith in Me that you finally let go of. That was all your worries of this world. All gone. It may not be what you want now, but it will be my will and I will never, my child, give you a burden you can't bare. You're going to have some really dark days ahead of you, days that will make you feel like giving up. You won't. And neither will I."

And so, this was the very Moment in my life when God finally started answering my prayers, OR, as He puts it, I finally started seeing that He had been answering my prayers my entire life, both big and small. Even prayers I had yet to pray.

"Eh, I guess we'll just have to agree to disagree, but I will tell you this, God."

"Yes," came the once again serene voice of a Father who now, in my mind, wore a smile of victory.

"Hey God, I'm still proud of You."

Big Mistake

She came back!
    I called.
    She came back!

Back in Time

And she kept coming. Every other weekend turned into every weekend. Little by little, both of our lives became consumed with our weekends together. I soon began to hate Sunday nights because I knew she would be leaving to go home for the week, and that would leave me with nothing but the fresh memories we had just created. The more time we spent together, the more we found out just how much we liked each other, and sadly, just how much the both of us loved meth. Every time she came to visit, our addiction would grow a little deeper. If I had been a better man, I would have stopped the madness right then and there. But I wasn't.

There are many things in my life that I am not proud of. This one is the top of my list. By the time you finish this book, you might just ask yourself; why would I even waste my breath on Devon. Why would I even try to, OR WANT TO, have a life with her. Just flip back to Chapter 1 and start reading and you'll have your answer. You don't abandon the ones you love, even if they did abandon you. Remember this book's dedication? It's our job to love them even when they don't love themselves. And if there is one fact in this world that I know to be true, it is this... I LOVE DEVON.

Every time she would visit, the longer our periods of going without sleep would become, which is really the entire point of meth, right? Stay up the longest to conquer the world, solve hunger in Africa, do the most crossword puzzles.

But the one thing you don't see happening is that you start disappearing.

We began to lose ourselves, little pieces at a time. Reality became a figment of our imagination. Nothing became important and what was truly important was ignored. Every tick of the clock put us just a little closer to our next shot of dope. Our own little slice of heaven. It was ok though because God was watching over us and would never let anything bad happen to us.

It's ok, God is cool with it", we would tell ourselves. "Because he knows we're doing the best we can do.

Drug addicts tend to spew such nonsense as that just to make ourselves feel better about having become such lousy sons and daughters, husbands and wives, parents.

Basically, just sorry human beings.

AND, it also helps to clear our conscious.

You see, the mirror is the mortal enemy of the conscious. It is imperative for a good junkie to be able to look at themselves in the mirror and walk away feeling good about what they see in order to maintain and continue in the fantasy that "everything is ok". We're not hurting anyone, and, in fact, have become a "highly functioning addict', who has everyone fooled.

"Yeah, right".

The only person you're fooling is YOURSELF.

Out of all this, I learned a very valuable and hurtful lesson. The lies we tell ourselves are the worst lies of all. You tell yourself everything you want to hear. You start believing your own lies. You're now even able to stand and look in the mirror and walk away with an actual smile on your face.

"Wow, I look good and healthy. I haven't done anything wrong. Everyone loves me and why wouldn't they? I'm a great person.

Keep smiling and those lies will eventually eat you alive and one day, maybe soon, maybe far away, you'll look in that mirror and everything and everyone you love will be gone. You don't even bother to ask for help and why should you? You've already convinced yourself you don't need help.

Those pretty little lies.

Anyways, what do we need help with? Devon goes home every Sunday night and is ready for work come Monday morning. I get up everyday and head out to work with my Dad. We both work forty hours or more a week. We work hard and party hard. Why can't we sit here on my bed and shoot dope if we want to. We're ok. We got this. Right?

Right!

"Hey purdygurl"

"What pookie"

"What day is this"

"Uhhh, Tuesday afternoon, I think"

"Shouldn't you be at work, Devon?"

"Shouldn't you be at work, Fry Daddy?"

"Yeah, I should," I replied.

"If it's ok with you, I think I'll just stay here with you," was her sheepish reply.

"Why not?"

"We're ok."

"We got this?"

MY God, my God, the lies we tell ourselves.

chapter 9

And So We Begin

Two months had passed and in this time, we decided that we should move in together. I remember we were setting on our bed the day we got all her stuff moved in. "Devon, I love you."

It was the first time either one of us had dared to speak the three deadliest words known to man. And I had to be the dummy that did it. She just looked at me with those deep blue eyes, smiled, and patted me on the hand.

"It's ok, you don't have to say anything," I said, while never taking my eyes from her. "You'll love me one day, I can wait." Little did I know that with those three little words, I Love You, that I set in motion one of the greatest love stories ever told. When she finally did speak to me, her question was simple and direct.

"Will you come meet my parents this weekend?"

"Yeah baby, sure. I guess it's about that time, huh?"

chapter 10

10-20-1 12:10 PM

"Detainee Fry, get your butt out here right now." boomed over the dorm loudspeaker.

What do they want now?

"You got a visitor, give me you I.D. and get up front", said the officer at the control desk.

I walked into the visitation room and saw my guardian angel sitting there. It was my number one cheerleader, my fiercest defender. The only woman who has never, nor will she ever, turn her back on me. My Mom.

"Hey Momma", was all I could get out before I began to feel the giant drops beginning to gather in the back of my eyes.

"Is everything ok?"

"Hey babe, I just wanted to come see you."

"Momma, what's wrong?"

"Sit down son so we can talk."

Going Home

"Hey pookie, you think we can do another shot before we head out to my parents?" "You know it's about a two hour drive from here to Newnan," Devon asked, slipping up behind me, dropping her left arm over my shoulder and then bending down and kissing me ever so gently on my cheek.

"How could I say no to that, baby?"

"You never can."

And so I fixed us up another shot of meth, we blasted away, and then headed out the front door on our way to her parent's house for my formal introduction.

Let me say this, if I were to describe us as being "high as a kite", that would be the understatement of a lifetime. WE WERE MESSSSSSED UP. We were not your normal, high as a kite high. You know, the kind of kite you see a parent trying to fly in the front yard with the kids. Oh no, not us. I mean, we were high as a kite as in a kite that's done got caught in a wind storm, ran out all its string then flew into the power lines, caught on fire and then crashes into the ground, jumps up, takes a look around to make sure no one saw what just happened, takes off running, still on fire, mind you, from the crash with the power lines, finds the nearest cliff and jumps off, because we were no longer a kite but now we were a two person hang glider...

We were high.

We were messssssssssssssed up.

For reals dawg.

chapter 12

Berry Ave

I was driving a Mustang SVO at the time. A very fast car to begin with, but I had put thousands of dollars into high performance parts and almost as much into a stereo system that would rattle the windows of other cars as we drove by. Just two more things that Devon and I introduced to each other. I showed her fast cars and she showed me loud music. We could rock and roll or throw out a rap faster than any two white folks you ever seen. We didn't care which one. We were young and in love.

"Hey pookie," I heard her scream over a pounding rendition of Bulls on Parade by Rage Against The Machine just as we got south of Atlanta.

"Turn it down, I can't hear you," I yelled back.

"What?"

"Turn it down so I can hear you," I yelled once more.

"Oh, ok" Devon began, "Babe, how fast are you going?"

"Bout 120, why?"

"I'm not complaining about your driving or anything, but you know those two 18 wheelers you just passed?:

"Yeah."

"You know one was in the fourth lane and the other one was in the fifth lane, right?"

"Yeah, so?

"Sooo," began her somewhat sweet, somewhat terrified response. "You were in between them when you passed them."

"Devon, I've driven in Atlanta a lot and this is the first time I am hearing about a lane IN BETWEEN two lanes. What are they calling this mystery lane, the fourth and a half lane?"

"I don't know Alton. Maybe we should name it Fry's meth lane of death."

"How close are we to your parents house?"

"Next exit."

"Thank God. I'm ready to get out of this car" I said with weary in my voice.

"Yes Fry, thank God indeed."

chapter 13

Meet the Sanderlins

"It's nice to meet you too, Mrs. Sanderlin."

"We were beginning to think that Devon was just making you up," said her mom, Denise. A beauty of a woman with a smile that went on for days. She had a tomboy short hair cut that suited her personality perfectly.

"I'm real," I responded. "I'm sorry it has taken us so long to get down here to visit and introduce myself." It was then that I noticed out of the corner of my eye a mountain moving across the living room toward us.

'You must be Mr. Sanderlin?"

"Yes, my good sir, but please call me Chris. I am, in fact, the fair maiden's father figure and you must be the gentleman she has been telling us so much about. A real life prince charming if we are to believe the stories."

"Although, I must warn you, you have some very big shoes to fill if you want to impress us."

"Wow, Chris, I definitely need to know what I'm up against. Let me hear it."

"Well, her last suitor just so happened to be a truck driver whose job was to deliver goods to convenience stores. He kept our house supplied with hot sausages, pickled eggs and a bad case of gas. He eventually fell in love with our couch and wound up losing his job. We came home one day and he had moved in his personal stash of sausage and eggs into our kitchen and claimed our living room as his own."

"Well, sir, I have a job, my own home and I hate both hot sausages and pickled eggs."

"I like you already." Was her father's quick response. "But you know the strange thing is that Devon has been living with you for about five weeks now, but he didn't leave till two days ago."

"We would tell him everyday that Devon no longer lived here and everyday he would start crying and blubbering, wanting to know what he did wrong, where she was and when was she coming back home."

"Before we could even give him an answer, he's stuffing his face with pickles and sausages, one right after the other. In between bites he was mumbling something about not knowing what to do without his comfort foods to help him get through this."

"As if that wasn't bad enough," continued Denise, "then he starts passing gas. We have this grown man on our couch, carrying on like a broken hearted fourteen year old boy who just lost his first girlfriend, eating the worst smelling snacks known to man, passing gas like his life depended on it. We had to do something," she finished. "Your father walked right up to him and said, 'son'.

"You really called him son?" Devon asked.

"Well, yes I did, Devon, but only because I couldn't remember his name."

"Son," I said, "we have some bad news," Chris began again. "Denise and I have not paid the rent in the last six months. We have less than twenty four hours to get out of the house before the police show up and kick us out."

"We don't have time to pack any of our belongings, not even our clothes. We are simply walking out the door and never looking back. As a matter of fact, we're leaving right now and we suggest that you do the same."

"And do you know what his response was?" Denise asked me.

"No ma'am, what was it?" I asked.

He said "Do you think I have time to finish up this sausage and pickle I just opened up?"

Chris told him "I would hurry up if I was you, and be sure to lock the door when you leave."

"Chris and I turned around and walked out the front door, got into the car, and went to the Chinese restaurant and had lunch. We went back home about an hour later, and as we drove down our street, we saw that his car was still in the driveway, but his trunk was open, so we just drove by and parked down the street to see what was going on."

"And" I replied.

"Well," Chris began, "for the next thirty minutes, he carried out boxes of hot sausages and pickled eggs and packed them into his trunk of his car, and when that was full, he started packing his back seat."

"He finally carried out his last box of snack treats, along with a hand full of clothes, got into his car and drove off."

"And we haven't seen him since," Chris finished with his hearty laugh.

"Wow," Devon whispered.

"I can already tell I'm going to like you folks," I said in my slow southern drawl.

Devon leaned over and gave me a kiss on my cheek and said, "I knew you would."

chapter 14

0-20-17 12:15 PM

I don't hear anything else my Mom is saying to me. My heart is beating like I just ran a marathon. My head is now pounding with an instant headache. I know I didn't just hear what I thought I heard.

No, no, no, no, no.

My Mom is still talking about something, what I don't know. I'm not really sure I believe what she just told me, but why would my Momma lie about such a thing?

Mom, please tell me you didn't just say that Daddy has dementia. THE FIRST STAGES OF ALZHEIMER'S. PLEASE GOD, PLEASE DON'T DO THIS TO ME. I'm begging you God. I'm not ready for you to test my faith. Please God, I'm not that strong. I know you told me you would always be there with me and wouldn't give me a burden I couldn't bear, but this piece of news is pushing the limits to what my soul can take. This might be what finally breaks my mind. I feel like God has just punched me in the throat. Sometimes in life you just can't find the strength to stop your tears as they fall. The current is to strong to turn the tide. This is one of those times.

"Son, are you listening to me? Did you hear what I just told you about your Daddy?"

chapter 15

Oh What a Night

"Uhhhh, Devon?"

"Yeah babe."

"What are these rats doing in your bedroom?"

"They're not rats Fry, they're hamsters. They're cute and fluffy."

"They're not cute and fluffy,' was my quick response. "They have pink eyes and long, nasty tails. Those things are rats."

"Cute and Fluffy are their names, and they're not rats."

"Holy cow, Devon, not only do you have rats living in your bedroom, but you named 'em too.

'THEY ARE NOT RATS," she responded with a mixture of anger and bewilderment. "They are clean, they don't smell. Here, pet one."

"Listen to me, ok. In the country, we call 'em rats. We don't name 'em, we don't pet 'em and we sure don't sleep with them in the same room with us."

"What are you trying to say, Alton?"

"What I'm trying to say, Devon, is that me and those two rats WILL NOT be sleeping in the same room."

"Just what am I supposed to do with Cute and Fluffy?"

"Uhh, throw them out the window as far as you can sounds good to me."

"I'm not doing that!"

"Okay, well then, how about this, take them and their cage and set them in the living room."

"My God, I can't believe your such a baby!"

"Baby? Baby! Listen here girly, have you ever heard of the black plague? Or the movie Willard?"

"Whatever Fry."

And so Devon picks up the cage with the two rats in it and walks into the living room where her parents were watching Saturday Night Live. I could hear her whispering back and forth with her parents, but I can't quite make out what they are saying. Suddenly I hear Devon's mother blurt out "Oh my God, really?" In his booming voice I hear Chris say "I'm really going to like this guy," laughing his hearty laugh.

"Ahh yeah, they love me."

Devon returned to her room, gently closed the door, looks at me with her wicked, sexy smile and says "Okay Fry, you're safe now. Cute and Fluffy are in the living room, their cages locked and I told them both not to bother you."

"Both, as in the rats or your parents?"

"The hamsters, you idiot."

"Okay cool, what about your parents?"

"I told them the same thing silly."

"Okay, I guess I can rest easy now that I know those two disease carriers are behind a locked cage and a door."

"Hey purdy girl?"

"Yeah baby?"

"Will you hand me my phone so I can check my messages?"

"It's 1 AM, can you just wait till the morning to check them?"

Now, if you will remember what I told you back in Chapter 3 about the life of a meth dealer so what I'm about to tell you should come as no surprise. Our night was about to go "not as planned."

"Devon, we have to go home."

"What did you just say?" Devon said with a hint of anger in her voice.

"Buddy just texted me needing a half ounce. That's $400. I can't just let that go."

"Can't he wait till tomorrow when we come home?"

"No, he says he can't wait, it has to be tonight."

"An just what in the heck am I going to tell my parents the reason why we are leaving their house at 2 AM in the morning ON YOUR FIRST VISIT?"

"Tell 'em it's the rats."

I always did make a good first impression.

chapter 16

10-20-17 2:20 PM Cowell PDC

I feel the first one rolling down my left cheek. It feels like a tidal wave, a natural disaster that's unstoppable, and it's just one single tear. But I know it's only the beginning.

"We took Papa for his VA checkup and they're concerned about his dementia. They have set up an appointment for him with a specialist next month to do more tests and a brain scan."

Why are you telling me this, I think to myself. There's nothing I can do about it in here. The last thing I want to hear is bad news. It was stupidity that put me on the wrong side of these walls, but news like this makes me want to get stupid again and find a way out of this place so I can be at my Dad's side just when he needs me the most.

Dammit, I feel another one bursting from my eye, rolling down my other cheek. In a place like this, it is much better to be tough and callous and be seen as uncaring than to be seen sad and crying and looking like you actually care about something. Right now I don't care. Say something to me and see what happens, I dare you. My Dad is in trouble, he needs me and I'm in here.

I hate myself.

I go deep within myself. I shut off the water works. God, my family needs my Dad. They need him more than I will ever be needed. If you have to take someone, take me. Do you hear me God? I'm serious, please, please. I can't solve this. I don't have a backup plan. But I am willing to bargain God. I will do my time here and stop praying for an early release and I will do whatever time you see fit for me when I go to court on the pending charges. I promise God, I will do all this and I won't complain, just give my father a clean bill of health, God. Take my time, take my freedom, take my future. But please God, don't take my Dad's mind.

Understanding God isn't necessary as long as you believe. I believe.

chapter 17

Like Kudzu

They say that life is nothing more than Moments. Some Moments last a few second. Some days. Still others may last years. Devon and I became a Moment that will last a lifetime. We were having the times of our lives. We had tasted the sweetness of paradise and at other times had the flames of hell burning our feet. We were living life trying to destroy the memories of old sins with the incredible madness of our new ones.

And we fell in love along the way.

We grew on each other. There would be times that we would fight like cats and dogs, but at the same time neither one of us wanted to be without the other. We were in the grip of mad love. We also had another love...METH.

Every day. All day long. 24/7.

Let me tell you something about meth. It is a vicious lover. It demands that you have no one but her in your life. It will wrap you in angel wings and make you believe you're on your way to heaven. She tells you how much she loves you and makes you believe it. Oh, how you believe those pretty little lies. And then one day you wake up alone, broke, broken. Your angel has turned into the devil, and

44

those wings that you once believed were carrying you to heaven have now drug you down to the depths of hell. But we still had each other and just like the kudzu that grows all over our property, our love kept growing and growing and nothing could kill it.

chapter 18

You Saw What

Let me give you a couple of examples of how people act on meth. We live in the country and being such, we have about every type of wild animal you can think of that at one time or another has crossed our property. One summer night Devon is standing at her kitchen window staring down our driveway when she says "Fry, come here for a minute."

"I'm busy, what is it?"

"Please, come over here right now! Hurry Fry before they leave."

"Before who leaves, Devon?" as I swiftly made my way to the window.

"Not who, but what," was her concerned answer.

I peered out the window and to my horror I saw, get this, four rabbits hopping around in our driveway.

"Okay baby," I said slowly. "I see some rabbits in our driveway."

"Rabbits? Rabbits don't have horns nor do they travel in herds."

"Let's go to bed purdygurl". I said in my best 'I know what's best for us' voice.

It seems that we had hit our stay up limit at 13 days. Yes, 13 straight days. Maybe an hour of sleep here and there, but for the most part if had been nonstop party 24/7.

"Fry, I don't need to go to bed," her anger beginning to swell. "You can't tell me that there are not dozens of rabbits with antlers on their heads in our driveway and front yard."

Let's not forget that Devon was born and raised in Atlanta. She had only been living here in the country now for about five months and was still getting used to all the wildlife we had around our house. Most wild animals will do the majority of their hunting, mating, eating, walking around, anything they need or want to do at nighttime, especially during the summer, because of the heat. Rabbits are no exception. They have a lot of fur and don't sweat, so it is only natural for them to be hopping around at nighttime.

Now, at first "meth" glance, these four rabbits did, in fact, look like a herd because all the jumping and hopping back and forth. When they would stop hopping they would pick up their very large floppy ears, which, and yes it is a long stretch, but maybe, just maybe when their ears were upright and stiff from a distance, they may have seemed to be a set of horns.

:Oh shoot, baby. You're right. Those are called Jack-a-lopes. "They're a crossbreed, half jackrabbit and half antelope! They still hop like a rabbit but have horns like an antelope.

Don't ask me because I don't know where I got that from. I just pulled it out of thin air. Actually, when you have as many voices in your head as I do, and they're all talking at the same time, its pretty easy to come up with something that sounds smart, ridiculous, weird, prophetic, hateful or even at time wise. Whatever the occasion calls for. What's that you say? Yes, you did read that correctly. I said voices in my head. How about we save that story for another chapter.

After what seemed an eternity, but was in fact only a few seconds, Devon turned to me and with a smile said, "Yeah, I've heard of those before."

"You have?"

"Yes, I have."

"Okay"

"I have more bad news Fry Daddy, we need cigarettes."

"Okay," I replied, "are you going to go with me to get 'em?"

"Are you crazy, I'm not going out there with a yard full of Jack-a-lopes."

"They're harmless purdygurl," was my quick response. "They're more scared of us than we are of them."

"I seem to recall about six months back, your very first visit to my parent's house. You, the big, tough, country boy wouldn't sleep in the same room with two pet hamsters. And now you want me to venture out into the dark of night with a herd of wild Jack-a-lopes in our yard? But I do want to go to the store with you."

"Okay baby, what you want me to do?"

"Go get rid of them. If they're more scared of us than we are of them, then it shouldn't be hard for you to shoo them away. I'm going to stand here at the window and watch. When you run them off, I'll run out to the car."

"Okay baby," I said as I chuckled to myself.

And out the door I go. I'm laughing to myself about the whole situation. I mean, I'm really giggling like a little school girl. I step off the front porch and head toward the front yard where the car was parked. I get about halfway there and start really noticing that, in fact, there are quite a few rabbits in the yard with flopping ears. I'm getting closer to the car but it seems that these creatures are not afraid of me. In fact, they seem to be advancing on me. I stopped dead in my tracks. Well, let's just be honest here. It was more like I was frozen with fear in my tracks. I didn't know whether to charge forward or retreat. The longer I stood there the more of my composure I lost. What was once a funny joke now has me in a state of confusion and panic. Are there really Jack-a-lopes? I'm now starting to doubt myself. Did I really make that story about Jack-a-lopes up, or did I read about Jack-a-lopes in some book. And then I hear it.

"Oh my dear God Fry, they're behind you now," I heard Devon yelling out the kitchen window at me. "They have you surrounded."

I turned just in time to see two baby rabbits hopping across the driveway behind me, which was all the motivation I needed to get my feet moving towards the car. Let me tell you something about myself. God built me to stand and fight, not run. But, on this night, I decided to run. And as I turned around to run towards my car, there he stood. The head Jack-a-lope. He was staring at me and I was staring at him. The only difference was that he didn't seem to be scared of me. I started inching towards the car and he started inching towards the car also. I start running and I mean I start running flat out fast. He started hopping just as fast. I beat him there, jumped in and slammed the door just as he hopped right on by. I looked towards the house but Devon was neither at the window or coming out the front door. And then my phone rang.

"Fry, I just saw what happened. I've locked all the windows and doors and I'm not coming out."

"I don't blame you baby, that was pretty scary."

"Call me when you get back and I'll have the door unlocked for you. And for God's sake, be careful Fry."

"I will baby."

I cranked the car, turned on the headlights and what do I see? Two baby rabbits. Two cute, furry, cuddly baby rabbits. I immediately had a flashback to Devon's two pet rats. I slammed the car down into drive and rushed forward toward the two baby Jack-a-lopes with hate in my heart and with the intentions of rabbit murder. I missed them on my first go-round, so I spun around for a second shot at them and of course what happens? My gas light starts dinging. I realize that I don't have enough gas to keep chasing them around the yard and make it to the gas station for cigarettes. By this time I am really needing a cigarette to calm my nerves after my harrowing encounter with the herd of Jack-a-lopes. As I'm driving away I make a mental note to myself.

"Self," I said, "get enough gas while at the store in case when we return home we have to chase these creatures around some more. For all you know, they may have called in reinforcements by the time we get back. Secondly, when you get back home, sit down and Google Jack-a-lopes."

That, my friends, is how a meth head thinks. ON A GOOD NIGHT!

chapter 19

NOTLA

Who I have become hurts me. I want nothing more in life than to be little Alton again. To never have done meth. To never have been arrested. To never have disgraced my father's name. But I can't turn back time. I can't undo what I have done.

Sometimes I feel dead. Will I ever be that little boy my Dad nicknamed "hacksaw" again? When he looks at me, will he ever see me that way again? Have I destroyed all the hopes and dreams he had for me? Have I destroyed little Alton and Hacksaw completely? What have I become? What will become of me? Dying has to be easier than living. It has to be. So why can't I give up on life? Why didn't I just take those pills I had in White County and get it over with? Why did I have to pray about it? Why did my prayers have to be answered? God, can I be the man I once was, before meth? Can I stop the hurt I see in my father's eyes every time I look at him? It sickens me to know that it was me, his only son, that causes him so much pain. So much pain and embarrassment for the man that has devoted his entire life to loving me, caring for me.

"Daddy, I'm sorry."

Dreams

I woke this morning and felt your lips on my cheek. "God, did I die last night? Am I in heaven?"

No, that stench is definitely Colwell Probation Detention Center. I'm still in hell. I miss you, Devon.

chapter 21

Don't Answer the Door

"Alton, Alton, get up."

"What is it Devon, I'm sleeping," was my grumpy response.

"There's two black guys at the door asking for you."

"What did you just say?"

"Listen to me," Devon yelled, "there are two black guys at the front door asking for you."

"What time is it?"

"What does it matter what time it is Fry, get up. Get your butt up out of bed and see what it is they want."

"It's 1 AM Devon, come to bed."

Let me stop right here for a second and explain something to you right quick. If there was one thing that Devon hated with a passion it was for me to tell her it was time to go to bed. If you wanted to get a cussing up one side and back down the other, tell her to go to bed. You want to start a knockdown, drag out fight, tell Devon she had been up too long and needs sleep. I, on the other hand, was in control of my mental faculties at all times. I acted no different than a normal, non-meth addict acted. I was a member of the upright citizens brigade. Or at least that's what the devil on my shoulder kept

53

telling me. I was a regular "father knows best." I've said this once already and this probably won't be the last time you see this phrase; the lies we tell ourselves are the worst lies of all.

I'm very good at telling you all about the splinter you have in your eye, while ignoring the 2x4 I have in my own eye. That's just one of the many evils of meth.

"Fry, I haven't told you the worst part of it yet."

"Let's hear it, Devon."

"They are driving a horse drawn wagon."

This got my attention.

"Not just any horse-drawn wagon. It's one of those old timey wagons that they haul coffins in. You know, like the kind they used in Princess Diana's funeral."

That really got my attention. So much so that I'm now out of bed with nothing but my boxers on. I get my pistol out of the nightstand and walk into the living room. We get to the front door and I tell Devon to stand on the side of the door and on the count of three, jerk it open so I will be facing them, pistol in hand, in my best cop stance that I can muster up at one in the morning.

One, two, three! There's no one there. Devon looks at me and says "go find them". Okay, that seems like the manly thing to do. And so I step out the front door onto the porch. Well, step is not quite how it happened. It was more like I jumped out the front door. I cleared left; no black guys. I cleared right; no black guys.

"They must have went around to the back of the house, Fry," Devon said with much concern in her voice.

"Lock the door back, baby. I'll find out what is going on around here.

"Be careful baby, they were both pretty big guys."

"How big," I asked, trying to maintain my best Don Johnson of Miami vice imitation.

"Bigger than you baby."

Wait a minute, I have a pistol in my hand, why am I concerned how big they are? Plus I have home field advantage. I'm really pumped up now. I slam my back against the outside wall of the house and start easing my way toward the far corner that leads to our backyard. I got a 3 day stubble growing from my goatee, I got on sexy underwear. I got my 9mm in hand and I'm going after the bad guys.

Don Johnson can kiss my butt.

I make my way, pause for a moment, and then I jump from the porch into the backyard, landing in my best Weaver stance, both hands on my pistol, arms locked out. I clear left; no black guys. I clear right; no black guys. I'm going back to bed.

I'm on my way back to the front door and noticed there is no horse-drawn carriage sitting there. You would think that this might be the point in time that a person might say to themselves, "self, maybe you should think about quitting meth." Your girlfriend is seeing scenes reminiscent out of the wild, wild west while you're running around in the yard at 1 in the morning with a loaded pistol, acting out your own action adventure movie."

Both of us are destroying our brains with meth.

That's what a normal person would think. This is what a junkie addict thinks.

"Man, that's some good dope. It's got me seeing people and things and then chasing after said people to possibly do them bodily harm."

If I only knew then what I know now. God forgive me.

I make my way back to the house where Devon is waiting on my perimeter check report. In case you're wondering what a perimeter check is, it's the name I came up with for my nightly walks around our yard to assure our safety. Just another side effect of meth; severe paranoia.

"Devon, there's no black guys anywhere around our house."

"Uh huh," she replied quickly.

"As a matter of fact, Devon, there's no horse-drawn carriage in our yard either."

"Really."

"Yeah, really,' I responded. "Is that all you have to say is really?"

"I can't believe you let them get away Fry Daddy. Maybe next time you should get out of the bed the first time I tell you that there are black guys at the front door asking for you."

"Wow, I think I need another shot of dope."

chapter 22

11-11-17 Colwell PDC 1 PM

I was expecting a visit today, not just from my Mom, but for the first time in 7 months, my Dad. He came up here with my Mom on the first visit but wasn't allowed in, because they said he wasn't cleared, even though they had told her over the phone the day before that he was. I told my Mom we needed to make this a short visit because I didn't want him sitting in the parking lot all day by himself. I hugged Mom as tight as I could without hurting her, kissed her several times on the cheek and walked her to the visitation door where an officer was posted up.

"Why such a short visit?" he asked. I explained the situation to him and asked him if it would be okay if my Dad came into the lobby while I stood out in the hallway behind the giant steel door that separates us from the outside just so he could see me and we could wave at one another. He said that would be no problem and Mom left to go get Dad.

When my Dad came through the front door and saw me, he didn't wave. As a matter of fact, he didn't even stop walking. I'm wondering to myself, what's he going to do when he hits the x-ray machine. I'll tell you what he did. He walked right through it, every red light going off and the man never even slows down. The officer in central control has jumped to his feet but seems to be frozen in place, wondering just what in the heck is this old man doing. My Dad never takes his eyes off of me. This man is on a mission.

I am in tears. My drug abuse has become my entire family's punishment. I hate myself.

My Dad is standing in front of me, crying. We are separated by 4 inches of steel and glass. But it seems like he's a thousand miles away. Anyone who knows my Dad can tell you that he had some of the most beautiful blue eyes you have ever seen. Right now, they're nothing but red. Red from the tears, from the pain, from the hurt. He put his fist up to the glass on his side and I do the same on my side. A father-son fist bump.

"I love you, Dad," I say through the thick glass. He can't hear me nor see what I'm saying to him due to his tears. My Mom is standing at the front door. I see she was talking and waving her arms, trying to get my Dad back where he's supposed to be. I scream, yet my voice says nothing. There's no sound. The pain remains trapped within me. I scream again. Still nothing.

My mind has become a slave and pain is his master. At that very moment, I wished I was dead and so I am bound and determined to make this visit different. Both my Mom and Dad are in the visitation room. My Dad has been cleared for visitation. I know from Mom's last visit that my Dad also had his doctor's appointment last week with his specialist about his dementia. I have been praying and praying about this. AND WORRYING. AND PRAYING SOME MORE. I walk into the visitation room and there sits the cutest couple I've ever seen. My Mom and Dad.

chapter 23

The Cold Hard Truth

I would not be doing justice to the truth if all I did was tell stories about how much fun we thought we were having. There was also a dark side. We both had serious issues. Neither one of us knew how to control our anger when we got like that. We didn't know how to diffuse the situation. I was the man, an older man in fact, 10 years Devon's senior. And yet, there were times that I acted like a 12 year old child. I should have been able to control myself better. We would get into a fight and Devon would be in my face screaming and my childish way of trying to shut her up would be a slap to the face.

No, I'm not proud of it. Yes, that does make me a sorry man. Yes, she should have left me and never looked back.

Instead, she would just wait for me to fall asleep or go somewhere and she would either steal dope or money, whatever was the easiest to get to and go have herself a party. It was an endless cycle with us. Sometimes we would fight for 10 minutes, sometimes for 10 days. I like to prove my point and Devon liked to punish me for proving my point. We loved to hurt each other, but let somebody else try and separate us and it would be hell to pay.

Looking back now with a clear mind and a broken heart, I see that it wasn't Merlin the magician that was helping to keep our little Camelot afloat, but in fact, once again, blessings from God that we chose to ignore. All our dope friends looked at us with awe. We were the power couple that no one could hurt. Our families, on the other hand, looked at us with pity. With total disgust and shame. We were the ones they had to love because we didn't love ourselves. Our addiction was killing us and we were loving every minute of it. This was the foundation of our destruction. Little did we know that were cursing ourselves.

YOU REAP WHAT YOU SOW.

chapter 24

Stop! Stop!

It was one of our typical fights. Devon wanted dope, I wouldn't give it. I wanted sex, she wouldn't give it. And so we went around and around. She would lie and deny and I would talk in circles. We were both very, very good with our own defense mechanisms.

We all have our own special brand of crazy. Devon and I were no different.

I think it was around 10 p.m. when this fight got started. We had been going back and forth for probably an hour when I thought I might try a different tactic. I gave up. Up to this point, there had been nothing but some pushing and yelling from the both of us.

"Devon, I'm leaving."

"Where do you think you're going?" was her very quick response.

"I don't know, just out for a drive."

"No, don't. Just stop," she said.

"That's what I'm trying to do baby, I'm trying to stop before this goes any further."

I started heading for the front door, with Devon right behind me yelling, "stop, stop, stop."

Once again, just another example of the evils of meth. You're in love, the next minute you're in mortal combat. Five minutes later you're back in love with each other.

Our lives existed beyond the boundaries of common sense. We were living somewhere in the realm of methdom, a kingdom of nonsense. Built on pain and suffering of one another. It would crumble everyday and we would build it right back. We decided that I wouldn't leave and we both agreed to calm down and just relax. I don't think we even knew what we were fighting about anymore.

AND THEN WE SAW THE PHONE.

No, not a cell phone, but our cordless house phone. I'm not even sure how the phone even got touched in the first place but somehow or another it did. AND somehow or another the on button had been hit...AND this is one very big and; AND not only had it turned on but somehow or another, it had redialed the last number! DEVON'S PARENTS. Oh, it gets worse. According to the phone log, the call had been made 40 minutes earlier, just about the time Devon was yelling "STOP, STOP, STOP...not, I mind you, because I was hurting her, but because she didn't want me to leave the house. Yep.

We looked at each other, not quite sure what to say or do. We were not even sure if her parents had answered the phone, much less heard any part of our fighting. If I was texting this to you, here is where I would insert an LOL, but unfortunately, we're not texting are we?

"Hand me the phone," Devon told me. You could cut the tension with a knife. I heard concern in her voice like I had never heard out of Devon before. "I'll check and see if we have any messages," she stated. Flash Forward into the future about 30 seconds. I could tell by the way her beautiful, sweet lips were beginning to tremble, that in fact something was wrong.

"What is it, Devon?"

"Shhhh"

I could tell by the tears that were rolling down both cheeks that we were in a big old heap of trouble.

"Oh my God. Oh my God. Oh my God."

"Devon, will you stop saying oh my God and tell me what it is."

"Mom answered her phone."

"And"

"Her and Dad heard us fighting."

"Uhhh, you better call and let them know what's up."

"No need for that Fry daddy."

"What do you mean baby?"

"What I mean is that they heard me yelling stop, stop, stop."

"Ok"

"They thought I was getting beat up and was yelling at you to stop."

"Well, call them back now and let them know the truth."

"I tried. They're not answering."

"Well keep trying."

"No need."

"What do you mean, Devon, No need?"

"They're on their way here."

"Where?"

"Here, you idiot."

"Your parents are leaving Newnan this late at night to come all the way up here.?"

"Yep."

"I can't believe this, are you sure?"

"Yeah Fry, I'm sure. Wouldn't you do the same if you got a call from Taylor in the middle of the night and it sounded like she was getting her ass beat by her old man and then when you tried to call her back, you get nothing but voicemail for twenty straight minutes? They left six voicemails, the last one saying they were on the way."

It was now my turn. "Oh my God. Oh my God. Oh my God."

chapter 25

11-11-17 Colwell PDC 1:05 PM

I'm very conflicted. On One hand there's nothing more I want than to finally get to see my Dad, give him a great big old bear hug and tell him I love him. Tell him just how sorry I am for leaving him on the farm all along. But on the other hand I'm ashamed of all that I have put him through. I'm embarrassed to face him. This man was my role model. A great one. He's been my best friend for 30 years now. True and faithful no matter how wrong I was he still had my back. No matter what stupid crime I committed he was my bondsman. I don't know why he never gave up. He had every right to. He loved me. I wore the mask of a good son, but for the most part, I was nothing more than your typical meth head. Selfish. Uncaring. Just a sorry human being.

But not today.

"Hey Dad," is about all I'm able to choke out before he wraps me in his arms.

"Boy, have I missed you son, it's been tough without you", he whispers.

He once had a voice that when he spoke you paid attention. It had a certain snap to it that when he said something you knew he meant what he said. Now it sounds wise, gentle, loving. What was once fear that made me listen has now been replaced with respect. That's why I listen now. Respect. And although he meant nothing by it, his first words to me in seven months cut through me like a knife.

My family is my saving grace, my constant tie to reality. Always there when I needed them and I know, without a doubt, my life would have been over a long time ago without them. Yet, when my Dad needs me the most, I'm not there. It comes time for me to stand up and be the man my family needs to lead them and I'm on vacation at Colwell PDC.

It is a poor man who has no honor. Right now, I'm flat-ass broke. I guess I'm living proof that all too often in this world, repayment for good is all too often bad.

"Y'all come back over here and let's sit down," I tell my parents as once again I am reduced to hiding my tears.

"You look good son," my Mom says and I guess she's right. Seven months off of meth and I have filled out to where I look like a human being again and not a skeleton. I am clean shaven, not even my signature goatee that I have had for 30 years. Even my fellow detainees tell me that shaven I look 10 years younger.

"Thanks Mom, you look beautiful as usual." My Dad, as anyone can tell you, is a handsome man. I'm looking at an 80 year old man trapped in the body of a 50 year old. Still blonde-haired and blue-eyed. A full head of hair of which I am quite jealous. I have inherited what is known as male pattern baldness from the Elrods, my mother's side of the family. Thanks, Mom.

"Papa went for his doctor visit," was the first thing out of my Mom's mouth. Papa is the name my two nieces, Amanda and Ally, and then my daughter Taylor, call my Dad. It fit him so well that everyone in the family just started calling him Papa.

"And what did they say?" I inquired. They're holding hands on top of the table. My parents don't do PDA'S.

"They said he was just fine."

"I'm just getting old, hack (saw)," my Dad said.

65

He called me Hacksaw. That's all it took. I can't hold my emotions any longer, but I have to. I'm setting in a room with 40 other cons and their families. I can't break down now. What I really want to do is jump across the visitation table, grab my parents up and run out the door with them. Never to return to this place of torment. Never to disappoint my family again. To finally become the son you need me to be. To be the father I need to be. To be the husband I need to be.

Instead, I ask my parents to go to the vending machine and get us some Cokes and chips. They leave the table, I bury a finger in each eye to stop the tidal wave.; It's just beneath the surface. I wipe my eyes hard. I shut down the tears as they return to the table.

"So tell me, what's all going on," as I restart our conversation.

"Well, the chicken company sent us a letter today and said they would be cutting out our farm sometime next year. We won't be able to keep our place without the income from the chicken houses."

God, what are you trying to do to me? Why is it one thing after another? I want to scream in frustration. I feel like I'm having an out-of-body experience. I'm once again full of rage. It's eating at my insides, I'm on fire. I feel my ghostly self rising from the chair I'm sitting in and walk away from my earthly body. I'm staring at my ghostly self, standing behind my parents on their side of the table, my vision from earlier returns. I see myself grab up my Dad and my Mom and tuck them under my arms like a sack of potatoes and we bust out of this joint. But, of course it is not to be. My Moms voice brings me back to reality.

"Son, son! Do you have any ideas about how to save the farm?"

I've learned the hard way that God can bring you down in a hurry. My mind hurts. My soul is tired. God, I'm sorry for saying this, but I feel like giving up. And once again God spoke to me.

"No, my child, you're not allowed to give up. I told you that you would have dark days and would feel like giving up, but I also told you that you wouldn't and I promised you that neither would I."

Welcome to one of your dark days, Fry. About time you showed back up, God.

chapter 26

Update 11-25-17 Colwell PDC

I hate this place. It's evil. Full of evil. There are demons that walk these halls. I don't mean the kind you see on TV or at the movies. You know, where Lucifer is a good-looking guy who does nothing but charm the pants off of women, or one of his bumbling henchmen who escapes from hell and is having the time of his life on earth. I'm talking about the evil kind of demon. There are men in here who are sick in their mind. Who do nothing but walk around all day and night thinking of ways to hurt someone. Whether it be mental or physical, that's all they want to do is hurt and destroy. Just a few moments ago, we had a fight in the B side bathrooms. Both young guys, one trying to prove he was the baddest in the dorm. The other just trying to stand his ground and not get run over. All the little guy was trying to do was to defend himself. His last words before walking into the bathroom were "I have a 4-year-old son at home. I don't care about you and I don't give a damn about fighting you, but you're not going to talk to me like that." The demon just laughed at him and proceeded to beat and batter him from one end of the bathroom to the other end until it was finally broken up. Not by guards but by friends of the little guy. The winner came out and was making his victory laps around the dorm, while the loser was getting blood cleaned from his face by his friends, who by the way, were not taking kindly to the winner's strut around the dorm. FIRST MISTAKE. And just like that, here comes his second mistake. On his next victory lap, he decided he wants to take a look to see just how much damage he had done to the old boy's face. His biggest mistake yet. He gets a little too close to the entrance of the bathroom and from out of nowhere another demon steps behind him from the crowd and shoves him back into the bathroom. Right into the crowd of guys who are still cleaning their buddy up. They took this as a sign of aggression. No questions asked. Like I said, this place is sick. The demon who didn't care one bit for the other man or his four year old son, has now just faced a pack of demons who have as much regard for life as he did. None. They beat him in the face till he falls. A pack of wild dogs who's feeding frenzy grows stronger with the sight and smell of their prey's blood. Like I said, this place is evil. They catch him as he crawls towards the bathroom exit, only to find it blocked. They're not finished yet. Still on his knees, he takes kicks that puts him back on the floor, urinating on himself after they finish. He now has two choices, lay there on the bathroom floor or get to the dorm door, hope you get the attention of an officer, explain to them that you just slipped and fell in the showers and need medical attention and pray to God they don't put you back in the same dorm. He had to have a little help to get there, but he wisely chose the door.

Every morning I wake up to the smell of bleach and no hope, a mixture that runs deep in this place. It seems to drip from the walls and ooze up from the floors.

God, I want to go home.

chapter 27

Do You Remember

Do you remember our time in New York City? It was the middle of January and it was cold. But, My God, wasn't it magical? We were so amazed by everything we saw. We walked to Time Square and saw buildings that reached into the heavens. We stopped at the corner of 59th and Broadway, possibly the most famous intersection on the entire planet, and we bought one of the world famous New York City hot dogs. You know, you always see them in the movies and on TV. It was horrible. Absolutely terrible. It was soggy, the color was off and it smelled funny. But it was a memory we made together. We went to Chinatown. Again, the very same Chinatown that you see on TV and in the movies. It was incredible. The shops. All the people.

We went to a cafe to eat lunch. We have always been adventurous, afraid of nothing and this restaurant proved it. It was a dive. This place was not meant for tourists. The menu wasn't even in English. The only thing that was in English was the prices. Us being us, we took this as a challenge. There was no communication between us and the very old lady behind the counter. We had to point to the things we wanted to try. We were so nervous. We didn't want to look like two hicks from Georgia. We had class, we had style. Some of the food was still moving (NO JOKE), we weren't going anywhere. We were the only people there. Which, looking back now, should have been another clue that we also should probably not have been there. But nothing scared us because we had each other. Not trying to sound sappy, but I don't care what was happening in our life; if we were holding hands, we were alright. We had seen worse. This is just another exciting challenge to us. We point. We pointed some more. We discussed. We ordered. We paid. We tried. We found a McDonald's. In the end, we had one of the most beautiful nights of our lives in New York City. We're standing on top of the Empire State Building. It was freezing. It was blowing snow. The wind was so strong it would cause you to start tilting if you didn't lean into it. Devon had her head buried in my chest trying to stay warm. If we had not already have been married, I would have gotten down on one knee, took the most beautiful woman in the world by the hand and I would have asked her to be my wife. But the way I see it, I was the luckiest man alive because Devon was already my wife. My best friend. My lover. My world. It felt like we were standing on top of the world. This was nothing short of a scene out of a romance novel. We just stood and starred out at the millions of stars in the night sky. It was as close to heaven as a person can get. I knew then that I had found the perfect girl and she was my wife. Only problem was, she thought she had found the perfect man.

chapter 28

They're Here

"Maybe if we turn off the lights and act like we're asleep, they'll just turn around and go home," Devon said matter-of-factly.

"Or, they'll think I have you tied up in the dark house preparing to do bad things to you," was my quick response.

"Yeah, you're probably right. I told them if I ever went missing that you had either cut me into pieces and dropped me in the chicken pit with the chickens, or to check the slaughter house in Mount Airy, where I might possibly be in the sausage.

"You're kidding right?"

"No, I'm not kidding, Fry. A girl has to protect herself."

Who even told you about the slaughterhouse, Devon?"

"Ken and Rea."

"Ken and Rea?" I asked.

"Yes, Ken, you dope man, and his girlfriend Rea. They told me that's where big mouths go in Habersham County."

"They were just kidding Devon. Jesus, no wonder your parents are on their way up here."

Have I told you that Devon's father is 6'3", 280 lbs.. And her baby brother is 6'1", 300 lb. Both very big men. I am 5'9", 200 lbs.

"It's going on 1 a.m. Maybe we should just cut the lights off Devon, like you said. Maybe they'll go away if they think we're asleep, that is, if they're really coming at all. They're probably at home in bed asleep."

Looking out our front door, I noticed headlights coming down Alec Mountain Road, which is about a half mile away from our house.

"Devon, I see headlights."

"Where," she responded.

"Coming down Alec Mountain."

"There's plenty of people that live on Alec Mountain, pookie. Wait and see if they turn on Sam Bell"

"They're on Sam Bell, Devon,' I yelled, interrupting her.

"Chill Fry, we still don't know if,"

"We have headlights coming down our driveway," I said interrupting her once again.

"Get into the bed and let's pretend we're asleep," I said.

"Okay," Devon replied. Both of us sure that this was all it was going to take to get her parents to go away. YEAH, RIGHT.

When Devon finally answered the door, her parents were beyond angry. That's kind of a simplistic description of what they were. More along the lines of enraged with hate. Her Mom had to stop somewhere north of Atlanta and wrap duct tape about Chris' neck to keep his head from popping off his shoulders he was so mad. He was a daddy on a mission.

chapter 29

I painted myself into this corner. I squandered what life had given me. I wasted God's blessings on things of the world. I have lost my career, my family, everything. I haven't been able to keep a single thing in my life that was important to me. No, not even my self respect. I sold it all. I was like a cheap whore, to meth. Even now, 7 months clean from drugs, I still find myself a prisoner. Only now, it's not just in my mind, but also my body, being held hostage. And now I know, no one can save me from this. If I could just go back to being little Alton.

I remember times as a child, all I had to do was lay my head in my Mom's lap and cry myself to sleep and all the bad things would be gone when I woke up. I have no doubts, not a single doubt in my mind that if she had the chance, my Mom would take my place at Colwell PDC. No matter how bad I hurt her, there's nothing that she would not do to stop my hurt.

I love you Mom.

I would love to be able to jump in the floor with my Dad once again and beat him at wrestling because I was the strongest 8 year old boy in the world. But I can't go back, can I? This adult I am hurts.

I have discovered misery, pain, and suffering. I have discovered life, I am told.

If I could somehow slip back into time to 1994 and stop myself from snorting that first line. Stop myself from buying that first sack.

Time is blind, Man is stupid.

chapter 30

12-5-17 Update

I must apologize once again. I really felt the need to write about my day here at Colwell PDC. There are very few windows in the dorms here. The ones we do have are about 6 feet off the ground and have a slight tint to them. It's almost like a casino here, except without the fun. They keep a constant temperature year-round. Along with very few windows, there are no clocks in the dorm. My point being, we don't have a clue what the weather is outside. But today was different. Today, I got to dream.

I wake up to yelling, which is actually the norm here. I sat up and asked my neighbor just what was the yelling about. He said they have clean bed sheets for us and are handing them out. I get up, put my jumpsuit on and got in line for one of the few pleasures we have, clean sheets.

I want you to just stop and think about that one minute. Your at home, in bed. Let's say you're laying there eating chips and drinking a Coke while watching a little TV before you doze off for the night. You drop some chips in your bed and when you go to clean them up, you accidentally spill coke on your bed sheets also. No big deal. All you do is get your lazy butt out of the bed, go to your linen closet, get some fresh sheets, strip the dirty ones off, put clean ones on, dirty ones in the laundry, and back to bed.

No big deal, right?

You may have just spent 10 minutes of your life to be able to live like a clean, decent human being. Sounds like a pretty good investment. Not here. We don't get that opportunity. If a drink is spilled on our sheets, "too bad, live with it, detainee," is what we're told.

Oh, and by the way, our laundry sheet days happened two weeks apart, end of story. You lay there in whatever filth you have managed to accumulate. They don't care. They don't even look at us as human. So yes, we tend to get a little excited about laundry day.

Each dorm has two front doors. One is the main door, and the other is the day room door, used to control overflow, like we have today. We walk out the main door, get clean sheets out of the big basket they have in between the doors and walk right back into the dorm using the day room door. Just think of it as a upside down U. Out one door, and in the other.

Right as I was about to re-enter the dorm, I just kind of stepped out of line a couple of feet to the right so I could take a peek out of the big glass door that leads to the basketball courts outside. It was raining. Just rain, but it was one of the most beautiful things I had seen in my life.

It was just a normal rainstorm, but I wanted nothing more out of life than to be outside in the rain at that very moment. I looked out into the freedom that the rain was offering. I pictured myself standing out there, my arms raised to the heavens. My head tilted upward to God so he would have to hear every word I had to say. Standing in the dry sanctuary of Colwell, I could feel the rain bouncing off my face. I felt the cold air at my body and embraced it like a long lost friend.

I felt free. I felt so alive. Instead of feeling like garbage, I felt human again. Just for a moment, a brief moment, I found a piece of happiness.

It was nothing more than a normal rain, but it brought back a lifetime of memories. I lived 47 years in a matter of what could have been no longer than 20 seconds. I thought back to the days when me and Daddy would be bricking a house and get caught in a downpour as we picked up our tools. I saw mine and Devon's old house with all the pots and pans we would have to set around the house to catch all the drips from the leaky ceiling.

But mostly, I saw us.

All the days we would wake up and I wouldn't have to go to work. She would roll over and just look at me and smile and say "stay in bed with me." And I did. She would lay her head on my chest and I would wrap my arms around her and we fall back asleep. I didn't care if my arm started hurting from her sleeping on it. I dared not move. I would kiss her on the forehead and whisper I love you, as we became tangled up as one. That's how much enjoyment 20 seconds of rain brought me today.

You may have my body Colwell, but you can't have my mind. NEVER.

chapter 31

Don't Answer The Door PT 2

We fought and we loved. We would hate each other, and then we couldn't get enough of each other. Everything in our life was out of control. Mine and Dad's masonry business was booming. We had work waiting on us. We had a good reputation in our community for doing top-end work and we charged as such. We were making a lot of money. Plus, my dope business was as strong as it had ever been. This is right around the time that "ice" showed up on the scene. Up until now, it had just been "crank," a less potent, homemade version of speed, whereas, the ice was pure methamphetamine, produced in a lab. It was evil incarnate. To put it bluntly; it was the devil. It would latch onto your DNA and it would change you at your core. The very being of who you were and it wouldn't let go. And I had the hook up.

Looking back now, I can see this was the end of everything I had known and the beginning of everything I was to learn. Little by little we lost ourselves. We spent money hand over fist. We were young and beautiful. We had it all. And then it happened. "Get up and answer the door," Devon said, still half-asleep.

"Just be still baby and they'll go away," was my reply.

It was raining that morning so I had the day off. On top of that, people weren't supposed to come to our house without calling first and no one had called that morning. The knocking at the front door did not stop.

"Alton, please get up and run whoever that is that won't stop knocking on our front door off and tell them not to come back."

"Ok, baby."

I got up, went to the front door, I had to go off on whatever idiot chose to ruin my morning. I opened up the front door to find not one, not two, but three dope heads. Wait a minute, these guys don't look like dope heads. And out of the shadows steps a fourth man. One I realized that I am very familiar with.

It's Chance Oxner, head of our local drug task force.

"Hey Alton, mind if we come in and talk?" He said to me as he didn't bother to wait for my reply and just came on into our living room. Our lives will never be the same again.

"Devon, get up. We got company."

chapter 32

3:00 AM

I got a letter from Mom yesterday. I love my Mom. She's one of the coolest chicks to walk this planet. She never fails to defend me, even when she knew I was wrong. Don't worry though, once we were away from my detractors, she would blow into me like a stick of TNT. Whenever I would hear, "now son, don't get mad at me," I knew I was in trouble.

Like I said, I love my Mon, but the woman has a knack for delivering bad news at the worst time. Well, let me just clear this up. No one, and I mean no one needs to hear bad news while they're locked up. ABSOLUTELY NO ONE. Especially someone who, let's say, might be on edge already. There is absolutely nothing a person can do about it here. You can't help them work through it, you can't make money to help him solve it. You can't go talk to someone who might have the remedy. You're nothing more than a helpless babe lost in the woods. Again, I'm telling you, Ruth Fry without question, is the greatest Mom walking this planet. A gangster granny. I love you Mom, but....I can't take anymore bad new and letters. The one I got yesterday told me the truth that I was sure she wasn't telling on her and Daddy's last visit. All his tests didn't turn out well. Your

Dad is having memory issues, the doctor doesn't want him driving anymore. The reason she told me that everything was fine during their last visit was because Daddy doesn't like talking about it. He doesn't want to hear what the doctor is saying because he says there's nothing wrong with him.

I AGREE.

No way in hell would I want to have to sit around and listen to people telling me that I'm going to lose my mind. That I will be unable to take care of myself or think for myself.

YOU CAN'T DO THIS TO MY DADDY. YEAH, I'M TALKING TO YOU GOD.

I feel drunk with agony just thinking about reading those words in my Mom's letter. I don't know if I'm man enough to face what might lie ahead for my hero.

Yeah, I know you told me that I would have dark days ahead, but I don't recall you saying anything at all about them including my Dad. It seems my entire life has been an endless loop of hope and destruction, of loss and joy. A story full of both pain and love simultaneously.

But, the insanity has always been just me, or me and Devon. I was always screwing up. But my Dad would be right there to help me up, dust me off, help patch up my wounds, tell me how much I was loved and send me right back up in the driver's seat and watched me go for broke again. Now it's going to be my turn to repay the favor.

God, please God, help me to be a good son. I have become pretty reliable at doing the wrong thing. I'm not looking for sympathy for the devil, God. Just some healing hands for my Dad.

I woke up this morning at 3 a.m. my face just inches from a block wall. I was trembling. I was scared. No, not scared. In shock. I couldn't help myself. I couldn't stop it from happening. I couldn't save my Daddy. It was just a dream, but I'm not dreaming these tears that are rolling down my face. I'm not dreaming this nightmare called Colwell. Nor am I dreaming that my Dad needs me. They're both very real.

I read somewhere that hope is the cruelest thing in the world. I'm in love with hope. Right now, hope is the only thing I am living for. Does that mean that I might be better off dead? I don't know. At least all this pain would be gone. But for once, I am gonna be a good son. I PROMISE YOU THIS, DADDY.

chapter 33

12-8-17 8 AM

It's beautiful. I've seen plenty of snows in my life, probably hundreds of snow days, but this one is different.

I've changed dorms since my first day here. Now my view out the windows is that of the outside rec cages. Nothing but chain link fence and a lot of razor wire. Off in the distance I can see a few snow covered treetops, but for the most part, I'm looking at a human dog box topped with man-eating razor wire.

But today, even all that metal looks beautiful covered in the snow.

It's now 6 p.m. and it's still snowing. This is without a doubt the most snow I've ever seen fall in one day's time. It reminds me of better days.

Me and my Dad are surrounded by Fry women. There's my Mom, my sister, Devon, my daughter Taylor, and my two nieces, Amanda and Ally. We actually went 45 years without a boy being born in our family. There was me, and all the girls until my oldest niece, Amanda had a handsome baby boy. George Alton is about a year and a half old. He's going to be a great man just like his namesake, my Dad and his great granddad, Alton Fry, SR.

Anyways, snow days are big events in our family. Our front pasture is big hill. Actually a great big hill from top to bottom. It's about 250 feet long. It's steep and fast on a good sled.

The first morning of a snow day my phone will be ringing off the hook. It's the girls talking Devon into getting Bubba (me) out of bed and getting up to Papa and Granny's so we could start our winter fun.

I would be in bed, sound asleep, knowing I had nothing but a lazy day ahead of me, or so I thought.

"Heyyy pookie bear, pookie bear, wakie wakie."

"No Devon, I'm not going outside to play in the snow," I replied without ever raising my head from the pillow. "You know I hate the cold. It hurts my feet." I would say with pleading already in my voice. "Besides, I smoke two packs a day, plus I'm a meth addict. That hill will for sure give me a heart attack this year, I know it. Is that what you want Devon? A dead meth head with a Marlboro sticking out of his mouth, halfway up that hill and half buried in the snow? Huh, is it? Cuz that's what will happen if you make me go out there."

"Pookie, I'll make a deal with you, okay?"

"Nope, no deals Devon. You can go play in the snow and sled with the girls if you like, I'm going to stay here.

"Just listen, Fry daddy."

"I'll listen honey, but you're not going to change my mind," I said stubbornly.

"Let's go slide down the hill and play in the snow with the girls for about 30 minutes or so, then come home and I'll let you strip off my wet clothes and we can jump back into bed and I'll let you warm me back up."

"Where are my boots?"

We loved playing in the snow actually. There would be times that Taylor would get to come up during a snow storm and we would seem to be the perfect family. We would all be outside. Me and all the girls in the snow with Papa and Granny sitting on the front porch laughing at us. We seemed like the perfect loving family.

One year during the snow, me and Devon took Taylor, Amanda and Ally down to the lower pasture in this Chevrolet Cavalier I owned at the time, to try and teach them how to cut donuts in a front wheel drive car in the snow. Amanda, my oldest niece declined my offer. She was always very serious, even at a young age. She was a very smart girl and still is. I asked Taylor, my daughter next, who, if I remember correctly, was a bout 9 or 10 at the time. She got in, started off and when she hit 15 miles an hour I pulled the emergency brake and around and around we went.

It scared her to death the first time I did it, but after a few times the concern left her face and it became nothing more than her and daddy sledding in the snow. Our sled was just a little bigger than normal this time. She did awesome.

Then came Allie, my youngest niece.

The best way to describe Allie would be to say that, much like myself, she was full of life. Very few challenges came her way as a child that she did not face and I'm proud to say that courage and excitement for life has served her well in her adult life now.

"Okay, Allie, just drive towards the end of the pasture," I began to say.

Ok, Bubba, then what?"

"Just listen to me for a second."

"Uh huh, I'm listening."

"Are you?"

"Yes, I'm listening. Can I please go now?"

"Take off, big girl," I replied.

That was probably the wrong phrase to use, because that's exactly what she did. She put the gas peddle through the floor board. This 13 year old kid had rooster tails coming from the front tires that had Devon and the other girls running for cover. She was doing her best to impress me, and I was grinning from ear to ear.

She's sitting on the edge of the driver's seat, one hand on the steering wheel and one hand on the emergency brake.

"Now Allie, what your going to do is," was all I got out, before she pulls up the emergency brake running 40 miles an hour.

Way too close to the creek.

When we finally stopped, she had one rear tire hanging off the creek bank, and I was staring straight down a ten foot drop into rushing water.

"Jesus baby, we're going to have to," was all I got out, once again not able to finish my sentence because this insane little 13 year old girl had done let off the emergency brake and once again has a rooster tail a-flying, heading back down the pasture where the girls are standing.

She's more like me than she knows. I could tell as we're flying back towards the other end of the pasture that her Mom is saying something. I believe, by the way she's jumping up and down that she might be a little upset at us. It's really hard to tell, though, because I have lost all my nerve for this joyride and have my eyes closed, but Allie has the gas pedal to the floor once again. This kid is giving car sledding everything she's got and I'm not sure whether the car or me can take much more of this.

"Slow down, baby."

"Okay," she says.

I don't know how fast were going when she pulled the brakes back up, but we completed three circles through the briar patch and had the girls hiding behind a tree, scared for their lives.

I cut the car off with it still in gear.

"How'd I do Bubba?"

"Please, give me a minute to catch my breath, okay?"

"I guess that mean I done pretty good, huh?"

"Uhhh, yeah baby, you done pretty good. But I believe Papa is going to be very upset when he sees how torn up his pasture is."

"Maybe it will snow some more tonight Bubba and cover it back up. That way you won't get in trouble with Papa."

"Maybe so, baby girl."

"Maybe so."

chapter 34

24 Hours

They find $75 worth of dope. That's it. I got lucky I guess you could say. The night before me and my best friend, Earl, went to go re-up (buy drugs). We got to Buddy's house, but no one seemed to be home. Just so you know, Buddy is a code name people use to refer to their drug dealer. It is just a name and in no way is that a reference to someone whose name is actually Buddy. Just so you know.

Anyway, Buddy's house was dark. No lights. No cars. He wasn't answering his phone, so we just left and drove back home empty-handed.

Once again, God was watching over me.

All I had was a small sack I had left at home and Devon had some pot. After they searched the house and found what they were looking for, they sat us down and started giving us the usual lines.

"Where do you get your drugs, Alton?"

"The drug stores."

"Your smart mouth is going to get you in jail," was one of the drug agents response to me quickly.

"I'm already going to jail," I replied.

"Not necessarily."

"Oh yeah, how's that?"

"Do you know a man named Earl?"

"You know I do. He's my best friend."

"Is that where you get your drugs?"

"Are you kidding me, he gets his drugs from me."

"What about his cousin?"

"Never met him."

And this went on and on for 30 minutes. Nothing in my answers changed, and then they ask Devon where the meth lab was located.

"What meth lab?" She replied.

"Our informant told us that Alton was cooking."

"Are you stupid? He can't even boil water, much less cook meth. That has to be one the dumbest things I've ever heard," she said smartly.

I want to stop right here for just a second. It's true that I was not cooking meth. I never have nor will I ever, BUT...

I just want it to be known that I am quite an excellent cook. I love to cook and have become quite good at it. More than just boiled water, too. Just sayin...

And so our conversation with the drug task force ended like this.

"We're coming back in 24 hours. You either have someone for us or you go to jail."

"Sure thing guys, but I'm going to need my dope back if you want me to go out. I don't like leaving home without it."

I never knew that sheetrock walls were really that hard until I got slammed up against it and told once again that my smart mouth was going to wind me up in prison.

They finally leave.

We sat on the couch, just holding each other, numb from what had just happened. After an hour or so we finally came up with a plan. We went to Walmart. We bought our first ever DVD, "Orange County starring Jack Black. We went home, lay back down on the couch and fell asleep in each other's arms. The most stressful moment of our lives had just happened. Our lives were crumbling down around us and here we lay, on the couch watching a movie.

We had been living our lives half the time running from God and the other half hiding from the devil. Sin came cheap and easy in our lives, but, as is the norm in people's lives that are running from God, we were about to pay a devastating price. And yet, there we were, in the safest play we could find to hide from the world. In each other's arms. I held her. I kissed her. I wiped her tears. We were as close to each other as two bodies could be. Devon fell asleep with me watching over her, holding our future in my hands.

"God, please help us." I wept.

chapter 35

Papa to the Rescue

True to their word, they were back early the next morning. They were upset at our lack of co-operation and so we went to jail. This was the first time that either one of us had been in trouble, so we were just expecting a slap on the wrist. They, on the other hand, had other thoughts. Our bond was set at $40,000. EACH!!!

PAPA! PAPA!

Le me back up a step here, they would not set us a bond due to a lack of co-operation. The sheriff at the time came to my daddy and said, "Mr. Fry, if you could talk to them and explain that a few names or some info would go a long way, we might tend to be a little more lenient."

My Dad, whether he'll admit it or not nowadays, was once, back in his time, quiet the tough guy himself. My Dad just laughed in his face and told her not to bother us until our lawyer got there.

Devon called her parents from jail to let them know what was going on. Her Dad, Chris, once told her that if anything ever happened involving the law in Habersham County to just call him and he would come up and put these hillbillies in their place. Yes, her Dad is a very funny guy. You can't help but like Chris.

When Devon called back home that night, her Dad had to explain to her that these hillbillies, which now all of a sudden he was calling gentlemen, meant business and they didn't give a darn who he knew in Atlanta, Georgia.

"Devon, honey, I love you and you are my only daughter so you know that I would do anything in my power to help you," Chris told Devon over the phone, "but these folks seem quite perturbed at you and Alton."

"What am I going to do daddy?"

"Well, honey, you better hope Papa Fry loves you as much as his son loves you, because that seems to be your only hope at this point."

Papa did. Well, maybe not as much as I love Devon, but he loves me, and she loved me, and I love both of them, so...

We bonded out four days later and returned home. Apparently, they didn't believe Devon when she told them that I was not cooking meth, because our house had been ransacked. They even tore the sheet rock off of the closet ceiling, leaving a giant mess on the floor, looking for a meth lab in the attic.

They went as far as to dig holes in various places in our yard, looking for buried money and dope. We had been set up by someone very close to us for them to know about my habit of hiding things outside. I'd like to tell you that this experience changed our lives for the better. It didn't. I guess it's true that a man who is drowning has no fear of rain.

chapter 36

Tay

Dear Taylor,

I can't begin to describe how proud of you I am. You're the type of child every parent wishes they had. I, on the other hand, was the type of parent every child is glad they didn't have. I'm not sure if your mother and I every really loved each other, or we were just doing what high school sweethearts were supposed to do. Get married, buy a house, have a baby. That's how people done things back "in our day". One thing is for certain though, Taylor, we didn't make a mistake with you. You were a beautiful, perfect baby. We used to have to take you riding to get you to go to sleep. I really didn't know what to do with you, but Jamie was never at a loss. I guess I was scared I was going to do the wrong thing, so I did nothing, which was also the wrong thing. I'm sorry, baby. Your mother and I just grew apart. She did things. I did things. We both did things to hurt each other. And so, we divorced. I went deep into the drugs. I was trying to bury my pain. The pain of losing you and your mom. The pain of not knowing what to do, being a failure. I wasn't very good at being a husband or a father. I'm sorry Taylor.

Even though we went our separate ways and hardly ever spoke again, there's one thing I can say about your mother. I could never haveasked for a better woman to be the mother of my child. I wasn't a very good husband or father and she wasn't a very good wife, but she knew how to be a mother. She loves you and knew exactly what to do. She never let you hurt or want for anything.

And as for her second husband, Tim, your stepfather, well, let me just say this. Tim was the father I refused to be. He was kind, gentle and understanding in ways that I could never imagine. He loves you just as if you were a daughter of his own flesh and blood. Tim, you are indeed a good man. Thank You.

Tay, do you remember a few years back when we were still friends and I texted you one night and I said, "the greatest thing I ever done for you was to keep the devil occupied so he wouldn't have time to bother you?"

You replied that you had no clue what I was talking about.

Now that you have grown a little older and have faced life head on, do you still feel the same way about that or do you know what I was talking about?

Baby, I'm so proud of you. I'm glad you were smart enough to learn from my mistakes. I wish I could have.

Love, Alton.

chapter 37

Back Home

And so, Papa bonded us both out and took us straight home.

"Devon, guess who was locked up with me?" I finally asked her once we were back home, alone.

"Who:"

"Marty," I replied.

"Our dope dealer," she asked.

"One and the same.""

"Guess who else," I continued.

"I'm afraid to guess, Alton, just tell me."

"Oh, it gets worse," I said.

"How could it get any worse than Marty being locked up and us not knowing about it?"

"Daniel was also there."

"Daniel, Daniel?" She asked.

"Yes, that Daniel. Your best friend's boyfriend had been locked up one day before we got there and we somehow didn't know about it either."

"No wonder we went to jail." was her reply.

"No joke," was all I could reply.

"So which one do you think it was," Devon said out loud.

"Don't know, maybe both," I said. "But Marty told me his old lady would take care of us when we got out. He was going to give her a call as we were getting ready to get bonded out."

"Baby, we just got out of jail, you think it's a good idea to go buy dope right away?" Devon asked me.

"Well, I don't know if it's a good idea or not, but I'm hurting for a fix." I whispered, as if our house had been bugged.

I could give you any number of excuses trying to justify my actions, but in reality, you only need one.

I was a junkie. And I was dragging Devon right along with me. We were leading our very own private revolt against manners. My parents had just put up $80,000 worth of their property to bond us out on drug charges and here we are going right back into the Devil's Den.

I was in the cruel grip of sobriety and I did not like what was happening to me. I had quit drugs in the past for much longer than 5 days, always under my terms. I quit because I was ready to quit. I could handle it because it was my decision and I was prepared for it. I wasn't about to let some cops tell me I had to quit dope. I had to feel whole and complete again, and there wasn't but one thing that was going to do it. I needed a shot of dope.

T.S. Elliot once wrote, "what you do not know is the only thing that you do know." If I could have only seen the future and the pain and suffering that was in store for us I would have never taken another shot of dope. But as the old saying goes, "it's easy to tell someone how to save a ship after it has sank." We were about to be drowning.

chapter 38

12-14-18 Colwell PDC

It's Saturday night and I'm bored. In fact, so bored that I decided to attend an AA meeting, just to get out of the dorm. No, I don't drink. My drug addiction took up all my time. I don't expect to learn anything. I don't expect to hear anything I haven't heard before. I'm just going there to pass the time. Me and a couple of buddies from my dorm walk to the visitation room, which is where the meetings are held. We sat down in the circle of chairs. The Host spends about 10 minutes reciting the AA mantras. After that, people began to speak and then something strange happened. I learned something. My entire life I had been under the impression that it was natural for mothers to love their children. Something that took no effort. But as the moments passed, inmate after inmate began telling their life stories. The more they spoke, the more I realized that all mothers, and fathers for that matter, are not created equal. I heard horror stories from young men, describing their first line of meth coming from their mother. One young boy even told us that his first shot of heroin came from his mother and father's sack. I realized very quickly just how blessed I am to have a mother like Ruth Fry. A woman full of grace and class. God gave me a treasure in my Mom.

Good Mothers are a gift not to be treated lightly. Both mine and Devon's mother are unreal. Mitch Albom once wrote, "sacrifice is a part of life. It is not something to regret. It is something to aspire to." That describes our parents to a tee.

My Mom is my number one cheerleader and my Dad is my hero. I'm telling you right now, if I needed someone to back me in a fight, my Mom will be there to back me up with her brass knuckles. And my Dad wouldn't be very far behind to bond us out. It's not that my Dad isn't a fighter, it's just that he has a reputation to uphold nowadays. He had his hands full trying to undo all the damage I do.

But you have to admit, Daddy, that in just a few ways I remind you of yourself when you were a younger man, right? Not the drugs, of course, but in the way you believe in standing for what is yours. Basically all the things a good man should do, but without the stupid, moronic things I added to it.

Mom, thank you for taking care of me and loving me. I have nothing but beautiful memories of our time. I love you and can't wait to get out of here and make you proud of me once again.

My Dad has been my best friend my entire life. We worked side-by-side for 20 years. You taught me how to be a successful brick mason, but you also showed me, by example, what a good husband and father should be. It's no one's fault except my own that I couldn't follow the path you had worked so hard to build for me. I tried to be a good man. Sometimes, the world just made it impossible.

chapter 39

Re-Up Time

And so, I called Marty's girlfriend and she told us to come on over, that she had us covered. No, you're right, it wasn't a good idea. Remember what I said about that sinking ship. Just out of jail on drug charges, the drug task force still hot on our heels, my Dad has $80,000 worth of property up for our bonds. No, not a good idea at all. But we were meth addicts. We were sick. Not only in our bodies, but also in our minds. We were in the grip of meth madness. And we loved it. Yes, it makes me sick also. NOW...But back then, we knew what we knew. We needed meth and we needed it now. I know reading this, that at times, our lives may have seemed like an adventure, yet at the same time, you can sense tragedy right around the corner, never far away. Looming, ever-present, on our horizon.

We showed up and this girl had lost it. She's so high and paranoid that she had spray painted the windows of their house black. Paranoia is just one of the hellish side effects of meth abuse. I don't care it it's your first time doing speed or you're a seasoned vet, meth will cause you to doubt and mistrust anything and everything and everyone. I've seen people convince themselves that a TV crew is following them around to make a documentary about their life.

Without their permission of course. I've seen people standing bare foot in 30 degree weather looking for shadow people. I've seen people peeking out of windows, yelling at Big Foot to go away and leave them alone. And now I seen this shot out meth whore paint her windows black and had convinced herself that she was able to see through the black paint to the outside, but anyone looking in will see nothing. Woman, I don't really care. I just want to get my dope and get out of here so I can do me a shot. I'm hurting. The strain of being without for the last few days had my nerve endings on high alert. The sound of people's voices make me cringe. The sun hurts my eyes. Breathing had become a chore that was making me mad. I am on edge and this meth addicted window artist has just pushed me over the edge of sanity.

"UH, bad news guys."

"I don't have time for bad news. I need my dope now," I responded in a manner that she was not accustomed to hearing from me.

"Well, uh, you see, uh, things have been a little crazy around here."

"And?" I say.

"So, well, uhhh, I thought it might be smart to get the dope out of the house so I went a few miles down the road and hid it in the woods."

"Okay, so go get it."

"I'm scared to right now."

"I'll go with you," Devon volunteered.

"How about y'all just come back tomorrow, we'll try then," she said without a care in the world.

That was not an option for us. After an hour of going back and forth with no end in sight, we finally came to an agreement that satisfied both parties. Her paranoia had set in so deep that not only was she not going to leave her house, but she wanted us to stay there and keep her company.

I agreed But in return, she had to call Dee, a friend, tell him where she had stashed the dope. He was to go pick it up and bring it straight to her house. I made the call for her and gave her the phone and she gave him directions. Two miles down the dirt road, turn left at the second oak tree, go past the blade of grass and walk 2 minutes to the north. Look for the four leaf clover, walk ten paces at a 45 degree angle and there it will be.

"This chick has done lost her mind," Devon whispers to me.

Thirty minutes later, Dee showed up. I'm looking out one of the few remaining windows not blacked out yet as he gets out of his car. I could tell by the pained look on his face that his treasure hunt did not go well.

"Did you find it?" Marty's girlfriend asks.

"No, I didn't."

"Yeah, I hid it pretty good."

"Well good for you," I replied.

"Just let me go get it in the morning and I'll bring it to you for all your trouble." she said to me.

"Well, I guess I don't really have a choice, now do I?"

"Don't be mad, Fry, I promise I'll be at your house before 9 a.m."

We had no other choice but to leave. We get to our cars and I turn to Dee, "So, you really didn't find it?"

"No, I didn't."

"Meet me down at Linda's gas station, okay?"

"Okay."

We get down to the gas station and Devon and I get out and walk over to Dee's car.

"Hey bro, drive back up there and let me take a look around," I asked.

"Let's go." Was his quick response.

Me and Devon get in with Dee and his girlfriend and take the five minute ride back up the old dirt road. We follow the directions to a T. We pull up, I get out and walk around for a few minutes and BOOM... there it lays. I pick it up, walk back to the car, and we drive off with a quarter pound of the purest crystal meth in North Georgia. We, however, did not go back to Buddy's house. WE GO

STRAIGHT HOME. WITH $6,000 WORTH OF STOLEN DOPE.

This was the first time and turned out to be the last time I ever stole dope. I may have been a strung out junkie but I was a proud one. I was proud of the fact that I worked to pay for my dope. I ran our masonry business during the day and my dope business at night. I didn't steal. I didn't beg. I didn't sell my belongings or trade them away to the dope man. I made my own way. So, this one time wouldn't hurt, right? Besides, she deserved it for not going and getting it like she was supposed to do in the first place, right? Like I told you before, addicts can justify anything. That's what we're good at. Little did I realize at the time that life-altering events, such as this, have incalculable consequences. It may take an hour, a day or even years, but there will always be consequences. We were about to find out just how so very true that last statement was.

chapter 40

12-22-17 Colwell PDC

I haven't seen the sun in 3 months. All the windows in my new dorm face north which, of course, means no sun. Yes, you can tell if it's a cloudy or sunny day outside, but as far as being able to bask in the glory of God's sunlight... NO.

The last day we had a rec call was the second day of September. The last wellness walk we were allowed to go on was the last week of October. Since that last wellness walk, which by the way is 70 men walking around in a square on the basketball court for 40 minutes, the sun has been nothing more than something I remember in my dreams. And yet, time keeps ticking by.

My entire life I've always felt younger than my age. Like I still had my whole life ahead of me. I've been comfortable in life more than once and lost it all, but it never bothered me or worried me because when I looked in the mirror I saw a fresh-faced kid who could do anything. Who wasn't afraid of any challenge the world had waiting for me. I looked at every day as just another chance for me to show the world I was enough man to face it and come out smiling. Now I wake up every morning and can't even recognize myself in the mirror. I have black rings around my eyes. My always tan skin has disappeared and left me with the tone of someone on chemo. My skin is flaking and my hair line is in full retreat. My beard now has more gray in it than any other color. I have become an old man. Scared and afraid Not because of where I'm at but because I'm scared and afraid of what lies in wait for me beyond these walls. I'm scared of life. I'm afraid to live. At times, I tell myself I deserve to feel this way. This is God's punishment for me and I earned it the hard way and this misery is my just reward. So just leave me the hell alone and let me enjoy my suffering. Could this be Karma once again making the world right?

Other times, I feel like the Prodigal Son preparing to return home, a stupid, angry man who has made enough poor decisions to really mess up his life. By some accounts, I should be spending the rest of my life in prison, or even worse, dead. Yet, here I am, given another chance at having another day to tell my story. The story of my life. A life full of wins and a life full of losses. Do I deserve it? Probably not, but I have it. And I promise you this. Mom, Dad, Taylor, Devon, Leigh; I'm going to make the most of it and make the most out of me. I've hurt you all, more than I will ever know. God saw fit to give me another second chance and I pray that y'all will do the same. I know in my heart this is my final wake-up call from God but just being given the chance is how I know that God forgives. It's how I know that God loves even the ones that some people may think don't deserve it. That's what makes me believe in things unseen. THAT'S FAITH.

chapter 41

The Beginning of the End.

I knew what was going to happen. Anyone in their right mind knew. I was, for the first time in my life, a thief. I was actually known to be a stand-up guy. One who never cheated and always tried to do the right thing by people. Not this time. We got back to our house, and of course, the first thing we did was to fix ourselves a shot. Zoom, zoom to the moon.

I had led myself to believe that I was conquering the world, and this free dope would be the thing that set me on my throne. I gave Dee an ounce, and kept three for myself.

"Listen Dee, don't go to town late at night and don't sell to anyone till I say so, ok?"

"What's the point of having it if I can't sell it?" Dee asked.

"Where you going to tell him you got it from?" I said. "We're supposed to be out of dope and now our dope man just got robbed and he's out. It wouldn't be very hard, even for these idiots, to put two and two together and figure out where their dope went to."

"Gotcha," Dee replied.

Dee left, leaving us there with dollar signs in our eyes and needles in our arms. I told Devon I didn't want to party through the night because I needed to lay down before daybreak.

"Why do you need to do that, pookie?"

"Because, this will be the first place crazy girl comes to once she finds out her dope is missing. As far as she knows, we don't have any dope," I continued, "so when she shows I don't want to be geeked out of my mind."

"Good idea Fry daddy."

"Yeah, I thought so too. So, you going to lay down with me?" I asked, already knowing the answer.

"Uhh, yeah, sure babe, I'll be in there in a little while. I want to catch up on some housecleaning first."

It never hurts to ask, I guess.

chapter 42

Hey Sandra

You know, you really think you're going somewhere in life, then reality shows you that you really have nowhere to go. God, I'm so tired of learning lessons...

"Alton, Alton, get up," Devon whispered in my ear.

"What?"

"Get up, Sandra is in the living room."

"Okay, okay. Tell her I'll be there in a sec."

"Hello Mr. Fry. How are you this morning?" Sandra said, walking into our bedroom.

"I'm tired," looking straight at her. "Glad to see you, I need some dope."

"Oh yeah? Funny thing, so do I."

"What do you mean?"

"I can't find my dope is what I mean," she replied.

"You wouldn't happen to know where it's at, would you?"

"Do I look like I know where your dope is at?"

"What about your boy Dee?" She inquired.

"No, he's not like that," I replied. "Anyways, if he had it, I would have it."

"Well what are we going to do?"

"If you'll give me a few minutes to get woke up, I'll head over your way and help you look for it."

"Okay, sounds like a plan. I had a little bit of my personal stash left, so I brought you a little bit of that to get you motivated," she said with a smile.

"Okay, thanks," I said. "Just leave it on the living room table. I'll fix myself one after I've had a little breakfast and then I'll head on over your way, okay?"

"All right, but you're sure you're going to come help me look for it, right?"

"Yes, I'm sure. I gotta have some."

"Okay then, see you soon," were her final words as she walked out of our bedroom.

I got up and went into the living room and sat down with Devon on the couch. "Let's look and see what she left us," I said.

I picked up the small sack and realized right away that it didn't reel right. I opened it up to look at it and the smell hit me right away. Powdered Clorox!

"Well, I guess she has no doubts about what happened to her stash, huh babe?"

"Damn Fry, she's pissed. That would have killed you if you had shot it up," Devon said.

"Guess I better start looking for another hookup," I replied.

"Guess so, Fry daddy, unless you like Clorox."

I SHOULD HAVE SEEN THIS COMING...

chapter 43

Faded Memories

My life has been a series of missteps that have all come together to somehow lead me here, the biggest misstep in my life. It's cold. It's loud. The people who work here are angry. Hate waffles through the air. Sin is the main attraction. All my fellow detainees talk about is who done the most dope. Who has the most money. Who has the most girls. Who has the fastest cars. On and on it goes. 24/7. There's a saying you learn real quick when doing time: be all you can be. Some of the stories you can't help but just laugh at. I've met a billionaire. He may have had a hope of people believing if he had stopped at being a millionaire, but, oh no, he had to go for the gusto and say billionaire. I met a guy who claimed he owned 20% of Microsoft, although he couldn't get his family to put $10 on his books. But that was ok, because he was actually happy to be in prison because he said he was safe from the people who wanted to kidnap him for ransom. I met a white guy who claimed that he supplied the Mexican cartel THEIR drugs. But the saddest and most pathetic guy I met in the last nine months was "that guy". You know the one I'm talking about. Always sitting alone, just waiting for someone to make eye contact with him so he can show you a faded photo of what he used to have. Who he used to be in another life. Begging for someone to care as much as he cares about thinigs that only matter to him. and then I looked in the mirror. My God, is that who I have become? Is that me? I picture myself through his eyes. I have become him. I dream of pictures of me and Devon when we were in Mexico. We're standing and facing each other. She had her head on my chest and I have my head tilted down, just touching the top of her head. It was a good day in our lives. And then I hear someone say "who's the picture of Fry?"

"The only girl I'll ever love."

I can't become him. I will not allow this to happen to me.

Sometimes I think that life is trying to beat my soul into submission To turn me into the coward I sometimes feel like. Not a day goes by that my thoughts don't haunt me. They seem to laugh at the man I have become. They torture my soul and are a constant reminder of the high price I'm paying for living life my way. My thoughts are like a schoolyard bully. They call me names. They pick at my wounds, wanting to hurt me more and more. Their laughter a constant reminder of my ever suffering soul.

Once again, I have become My Own Worst Enemy. My body locked in mortal combat within itself. I am in civil war. IT'S ME AGAINST ME. Please God, help me. Please God, just stop all of this. The heart lies and the head plays tricks on us, but the eyes always see the truth. Sometimes it's just hard to face it. But I'm learning.

chapter 44

The Best Job I Ever Had

For 16 years I felt it was my job to take care of and provide for Devon. It was more than my job...IT WAS MY LIFE. To care for her, to keep her safe, to make her happy. I didn't want her to know the pressures or stress of life. She didn't have to worry about the house payment. No worries about car insurance or how our groceries got paid for. I wanted life to be happy and beautiful for her. She became the woman I couldn't live without. That once in a lifetime love. That inferno that burned so hot that nothing could touch it. You can't fake the connection we have. Our love did, IT DOES, go beyond the physical, beyond the spiritual. When I laughed, she laughed. When she cried, I cried. When we looked at each other, I saw forever. I lived to make her smile. When we were wrapped in each other's arms, you could feel that "once in a lifetime." Some people want to say that we were living life looking through rose colored glasses. Maybe so. But we didn't care. Devon knows who, and what, exactly I am. And I know the same about her. And, despite that, we still loved each other. So no matter what people tell me or want me to think, I will always believe in us... I have to. I suppose I'm growing up, or maybe I'm just growing old. Either way, I've learned that loss changes a man.

Sometimes for the good. Most often, for the worse. Loss hurts. It scars. It destroys. But with that destruction comes a silver lining. A CHANCE TO REBUILD, DREAM A NEW DREAM. The pain of losing will always be stronger than the joy of winning. That's just the way life is. But it gives you something to hope for. And one thing in my life is for certain...I AM IN LOVE WITH HOPE.

chapter 45

Says He Would

That was the last time we ever saw Sandra. Never heard a word out of Marty when he got out of jail either. But our biggest problem still loomed ahead, coming up quick on the horizon. It had been 5 days since Sandra had left our house and I still had yet to locate a new "plug". Although I had told Dee to stay out of sight after the incident at the house, I said the heck with it and started to let the dope flow and we were now down to just a sack for our personal use.

In steps none other than my old friend John, my longtime friend and cohort, who just so happens to be laid up with a dope whore in Stockbridge, Georgia, only about 10 minutes from where Devon's family lived in Rex, Georgia.

"Call your Mom and Dad and tell 'em we're coming down for the weekend," I tell her.

"Okay pookie," she replied.

We go to her parents for the weekend and have a great time as usual. I called John on Sunday, he gave us directions and we went to go meet him at the trailer park where he was staying. We get there, meet the chick he's shacked up with, tell her we want an ounce and off she goes up toward the other end of the trailer park with my money in hand. She returns about 30 minutes later with some pink crank, the same subpar dope we were getting a year ago in Habersham before the crystal meth showed up. There was nothing I could do. I had already paid for it, and in the dope game, there are no refunds or an exchange policy. You get what you get.

We fixed ourselves a shot, said our goodbyes and headed back to Devon's parents. We get back, pack our stuff and tell her parents we would see them in a couple of weeks. A few weeks before this, Devon had went down one day to her parents without me. She had driven our other car, the one we had taught the girls how to drive in snow. It was a piece of junk that got her down there, but of course wouldn't crank when she got ready to come home, so I was tasked to come down and pick her up in the Mustang. In the few weeks that had passed between visits her brother had fixed the problem for us. When we left this time, we had us a mini convoy Me in the front and Devon behind me. We were cruising down Interstate 285 when we were supposed to merge onto 85 north. I made it. Devon did not.

"What are you doing," I asked as she answered her cell phone.

"I was playing with the radio"."

"I'm getting off the next exit now, I'm turning around. I won't be 10 minutes behind you," she replied.

"Okay, cool," I said. "So you don't need me to pull over and wait?"

"I grew up in Atlanta, Fry daddy. "I know the way home."

"I love you."

"I love you too."

So I kept driving, but the further I drove the more I wanted to do another shot of dope. And so, while driving with one hand, I fixed myself another blast of dope. Using my knees to drive, I shot up while driving down Interstate 85 running about 90 miles an hour.

Life in the Fast Lane....

About halfway home, somewhere I would say, around Buford, I began to feel it in my legs. No matter how much I tried to ignore it, I knew what this feeling was... I HAD TRASH FEVER.

Trash fever occurs when you've gotten dope that's been cut with poison, or your careless when your making up your shot and you don't filter it properly. The best description I can give you of what trash fever is, is this; a very painful death that most people live through. Not all.

A year before this, my Dad and I had this young man working for us as a laborer in our masonry business. Strongest kid I've ever seen. He had a wife and two little kids. He also had a meth habit and in the end, trash fever was what killed him. After three days in a coma, he dies, still so swollen from the poison that they had to have a special casket made for him. Me and Devon went to see him at the hospital. We walked in his room, took one look and walked away. We were not prepared to face the reality of what meth looks like when things go bad. It was sickening. His face puffed up, his body looking like a dead animal that had ballooned to epic proportions, any moment ready to explode. After leaving his room, we drove home and did the only thing that we knew to do...A SHOT OF DOPE.

chapter 46

The Long Ride Home

"Hey Baby," Devon said as she answered her phone "What's up?"

"I think I have trash fever," I say to her.

"Oh my God, are you sure?"

"Pretty sure," I reply, trying to steady my voice.

"Pull over and wait on me to catch up with you so I can drive the rest of the way home."

"I'm already past Gainesville. I think I can make it."

"If you get worse baby, pull over and wait on me, okay?"

"I will, but I'm putting it in the wind a little to try and get home before it comes on full force."

"Not too fast, baby," Devon said. "Remember you got an ounce of dope in the car with you."

"I'll be careful. I love you and I'll see you at home," I said, hanging up my phone.

I don't remember making it home. I don't know how long I've been sitting there in my car before Devon found me.

"Alton, Alton, oh my god baby, we got to get you to the hospital."

"No hospitals, Devon. Mama and Daddy will find out."

"I don't care if they do, baby, you're dying," Devon said through a river of tears.

"I do care," I yelled. "Take me to Scottie and Lizzie's, he'll know what to do."

The rest is a blur. I remember Scotty and Devon getting me out of the car at his house. I remember moments of screaming in pain. I thought I was on fire. I was convulsing, my body jerking with spasms that I could not control.

"God, please save me. I don't want to die like this."

I remember waking up, lying in one of Scotty and Lizzy's spare bedrooms. I was sure a train was running through the middle of my head. It was pounding, beating, screaming. I had lost all control of my muscles. My body jerked so bad from the spasms that I was sure I was breaking bones or tearing muscle tissue. But in fact, I was being held by an Angel. My angel. Devon. She was lying behind me and had her arms and legs wrapped around me trying to keep me from hurting myself from the constant twitching of my muscles. Right now, as I'm writing this, I can still feel her lips kissing my neck, her tears cooling my body with ever one that fell. I remember her telling me how much she loved me and to hold on.

"Alton, don't do this to me. I need you, pookie."

"I can't live without you," I remember hearing her whisper as I began to fade away.

My last memory was of Devon and Scotty placing bags of ice on my stomach and chest along with cold rags on my face in an attempt to lower my fever.

"Please God, don't let me die. Not like this."

PLEASE...

"My parents have already lost once child, my sister, Theresa. Please don't make Devon have to tell them that they have now lost their only son.. God? GOD?"

chapter 47

12-24-17 Colwell PDC

Sunday is the worst day of the week here at Colwell PDC. It's football season and that's all that is on the TV from noon time when the pre-game show starts all the way up to 11 p.m. lights out. It's loud. VERY LOUD. You have grown men screaming at a 19 inch TV screen like they have a million dollar bet on the outcome, instead of a honey bun. I hate the screaming. I hate the people screaming. I hate the TV. I know God, I'm trying. I'm trying. In the last 10 months I have learned so much about hate. It is a deadly poison, a disease that always kills in the end. The sad truth to such an ending is that most of the time, you're the one who winds up dead. Sometimes it's just your soul dying. Other times, it takes everything. One way or the other, in the end, it will eat you alive.

Have you ever found yourself in the grip of anger so strong you literally didn't know what to do? That's the way I felt today. It just kept getting louder and louder. Twice the guards came into our dorm and gave us warnings to keep it down or they would cut off the TVs and the phones for the day. I pray to God to help me not hate, to not be angry, to be able to maintain my inner peace and happiness that I have prayed so hard to find. You know, sometimes all a person needs is just a sign from God, just to let us know he is still there. And then I got mine.

"Those wishing to attend Christmas Eve church services, line up at your front door."

Hating so bad all day long on things that I have no control over, I had overlooked the fact that we got church today. I've been sitting here feeling sorry for myself having to live like this, and didn't realize that I was allowing bitterness to steal and destroy my joy. Instead of praying to God to help me overlook the things that were bothering me and to help me carry on, I was cursing under my breath, mumbling to myself about what I would like to do with that TV. Once again, like so many other times in my life, instead of going to God in prayer, I just got angry. And then I heard that announcement. Thank you, God. We lined up and headed down the hall to the visitation center, which is also our church, also the intake center for new inmates and on Friday and Sunday nights, the room for the AA meetings. It is, without a doubt, the most used room in Colwell.

I'm going to be completely honest with you here. I wasn't really in the mood for church today. I just wanted to be lazy. I wanted to stay in my bunk and just listen to all the noise that has been driving me crazy all day just so I would have something to grumble about, I guess. But, as so many other times in my life, God's plans were not the same as mine. By the time the service was over, I was in tears. Not my usual tears of pain or worry, these were of joy. These joyful tears were coming from my renewed heart. I was hungry and had been fed. My spirit and soul renewed. I could breathe once again. I hadn't asked God for a sign just to let me know he was still there; but that's the beauty of God. I DIDN'T HAVE TO. He knew what I was needing. My God, my God. What a great and beautiful God you are.

Just 10 minutes away from another Christmas gone wrong. This year I'm locked up. Last year Devon and I got divorced before Christmas. Two years ago Devon was locked up. Four years ago I was locked up in Habersham county during Christmas. Six years ago Devon and I were separated. December hasn't been a very good month for us.

It's getting loud again. Even louder than before. It's cool, though. I got fed with God's word. I prayed for my own island of peace and I found it. There's no one here except for me and God.

"Lights out in 5 minutes."

Sure is still loud in here. And here they come.

"Everyone in your own rack now," one officer screams. "I'm taking your TVs for tomorrow and if you don't shut your mouths, I'll take your phones. That will be Christmas day with no TVs and phones."

Just so you know, I left out about 400 cuss words. Please don't go thinking that the guards speak to inmates that politely.

Everyone quietens down. Almost everyone. There are no shortage of dorm clowns, and sure enough, one steps up to the plate with a comment that enrages an already mad officer.

He stops at the door, "there goes your phones. Merry Christmas," as he slams the dorm door behind him. The dorm clown steps back up to the plate again for another swing.

"Well they done took our TV and phones for tomorrow so I guess that means that we can now raise hell since we ain't got nothing left to lose, and all hell broke loose for about 5 minutes until they got the sergeant on duty and back up in place and then they all came in. A lot of screaming, a lot of yelling, a lot of pushing and shoving and threats about this and that. In the end, as is the norm, the guards won out and order was restored. Not a very good start to Christmas. I don't think Santa will be stopping by here tonight. I don't think it would be safe. I'm pretty sure he would get drug into B side bathrooms and beat up, his sack of goodies looted and then left for dead. Best to just keep on moving, Santa. MERRY F***ING CHRISTMAS...

chapter 48

God

I'm awake. I think I am but something isn't right. This looks like my bedroom but I'm not sure it is really is. Am I alive? Did I survive my battle with trash fever or have I paid the ultimate price? I've spent the last 10 years of my life holding the needle like a gun in my hand, daring myself to pull the trigger, not caring whether or not this just might be the time that I pay the ultimate price for the pleasure of that little pin prick.

Just calm down I tell myself. Take a few minutes to gather your composure and try to figure things out. Something's not right. Why am I so scared? There's something missing. I can feel it. Or rather, I can't feel it. The presence. The feeling of comfort and deep love. The presence. His presence. It's missing. It's no longer there. GOD HAS LEFT ME. Am I dead? Is this hell? I am frozen on my bed, afraid to move. Afraid to speak or call out. My mind is flooded with a million thoughts, a life time of memories that I am not even sure are my own. Death is the end of Hope. I feel that for sure. Death is a friend when you have lost all hope for friendship. Right now, I feel like all hope is lost. Maybe I couldn't find my way to the light. Maybe I saw only misery and sadness in the light and decided to follow death into the darkness. Maybe death will bring me comfort in a Most Blessed Way. NO... That's not really how I feel. That's not what I asked for. I feel like a lost child who can't find his parents. I didn't ask for death. I ASKED YO TO SAVE ME GOD. No one wants to die, no one wants death, no matter how severe or grotesque our suffering may be. All we really want is just some relief. For all the pain to go away, to stop the torment, to once again find a life of happiness and love. I have just learned death is not sweet. Death hurts. It's scary. It truly is the end of Hope. Without God, without his loving presence, my life just changed. I awoke a living dead man. I feel my body began to shake as I break out in tears. The pain in my soul too powerful to even try to stop my emotions. I have to find my voice. I need help.

"DEVON, DEVON," I scream through my tears, which have now devolved me into a ball of raw nerves and frightened tremors.

She comes running into the bedroom and instantly burst into tears when she sees the condition I'm in.

"I'm here baby, I'm here," she says trying to comfort me.

There are no words adequate enough to describe this moment. She wrapped her arms around me as I screamed and cried, begging her to comfort me. She is at a loss for words. My pain is not understandable to any one except me. GOD IS NO LONGER IN ME. My world suddenly seemed no more real than a dream. I kept telling myself to wake up. WAKE UP. Just open your eyes and this nightmare of emptiness will be over. I was awake. This was no dream, but it was definitely a nightmare.

chapter 49

Sleep

All I want to do is sleep. I just want to wake up and it be my release date of February 9th. I've never had good sleep habits, and even though I've been meth free going on a year now, I still have trouble sleeping. I've spent many sleepless nights, both here and at home, when I thought the promise of a new day would never come. Being locked up has just magnified my sleep issues. This place gives you no purpose, nothing to hold on to. I lay here at night and I can't shut my mind off. Thoughts, memories, both race through my head, never giving me a moment's rest. I replayed what happened a year ago, 5 years ago, thinking if I had done this or that maybe the outcome would have been different. I can't change the past, but I can't get out of it either. I'm driving myself insane. When I do get the civil war in my head down to a dull roar, I just lay here trying to listen to the sound of my heartbeat, wondering, praying to God to show me the way. To just reassure me that the struggle is still worth it. I just want peace in my life. If I could just sleep 24 hours a day for the next month and a half, I would be a happy man. But I know I can't.

When I do sleep, I dream of Devon. She is always smiling. A smile that makes the sun jealous. She looks at me and all my worries and cares fade away. It feels like pure oxygen. If I could capture this moment, I would never have to do meth again. She's the greatest drug I have ever done.

When I can't sleep, which is most of the time, I lie awake and stare at the block wall just a few inches from my face, or straight up at the bed above me. Quite a stark contrast of when I couldn't sleep at home. Sometimes I would lay awake at night and just watch over Devon, amazed at her beauty. I couldn't help but smile at her naked splendor. She was a goddess I had discovered while exploring the world. She was mine to worship. I loved her. I love her. And now, the same memories that I once cherished and clung to as my security blanket are now the things that keep me awake at night and torment my very being.

We're not allowed to sleep during the day, so the daytime is no better. I try to busy myself with my job at the library to keep my mind off of my other life, but every day turns into a struggle of unearthly strength to turn my thoughts away from my losses, my freedom, my family, my future. I just can't turn it off. I simply cannot give myself a moment of peace or rest. It's an endless loop of film replaying my life's greatest gaffes. All my mistakes and all my failures. But worst of all, it also contains all the things that I did right. All my cherished moments with my parents, all the fun trips with Taylor and the girls, my masonry business, my beautiful home, all gone, thrown away. Because I chose meth over the blessed life God had given me. There are still times I lie here and contemplate suicide.

But that would be the easy way out and God is not going to let me take the easy way out.

"Are you Buddy?"

One day, when I'm an old man, I will forget what I want to remember. But for now, I am cursed to remember what I want to forget.

Just Tell Me

I have lost total control of my emotions. I feel nothing but sheer terror.

"Devon, something's missing," I cried.

Please baby, just tell me what it is and I'll go get it for you."

"Something's gone."

"What is it honey? You want something to eat or drink, just tell me baby."

It's God."

"What do you mean God, what about God?" She said through her own storm of confusion and tears.

"Devon, God has left me."

"What?"

For the first time of my life, I don't feel God's presence within me.

"He's left me," I scream.

40 years ago, I heard the same scream.

I was 8 years old, still just a child by all measure. I was lying in bed one night when I was awoken by screaming. I got out of bed and remember crawling on my hands and knees down the hall. I peeked around the corner, and down stairs was my Mom, being held up by my Daddy and my uncle J.R., her brother. Standing in front of her were two policemen, both silent statues. She was screaming and crying, repeating no, no, no over and over again. I stayed for only a moment before I returned to the safety of my bed. I didn't know why, nor could I understand just why my Mama was so mad at Daddy and Uncle J.R. that she would be screaming and crying at them.

I didn't think they would hurt her with the police there. All I knew was that I didn't like hearing my Mom cry. I just knew I didn't want to be there anymore so back to my room and back to bed before I was noticed.

The next day it was explained to me that Teresa, my oldest sister, wouldn't be coming home again. She had been killed in a car wreck on her way home from work. 18 years old, beautiful and alive one minute, and the next minute, my Mom is cursing God and asking why. Asking the same question that I was now asking myself... WHERE ARE YOU GOD??

Devon and I sat together and cried. She explained to me that I had been in the bed for almost 4 days now. I spent a day and a half at Scotty and Lizzie's before I was able to move, at which time they got me to the car and then brought me home 2 days ago. She tells me she covered me being out of work with Daddy by telling him that I was sick. Then she gave me one of her makeup mirrors because I needed to see something. I threw up so much stomach acid that my lips and skin around my mouth were blistered. Both were red and flaking. I was an absolute disaster. Both mentally and physically.

I couldn't let go of Devon. I just buried my head in her chest and cried. I was afraid to move. I knew beyond a shadow of a doubt that I was all alone. In my religion I was taught "once saved, always saved", but at this very real moment in my life, I felt if I were to die, I would surely open my eyes in Hell. I take that back. At that very moment, I WAS ALLOWED TO TASTE HELL. I was being given a very real glance into what lay ahead for me.

I read once that hell is waking up and realizing that you chose wrong and that when you cry out for God, he doesn't answer. Just the same way you didn't answer him on Earth. You will be spending an eternity crying out to God, knowing he's there, but will never answer you. Nothing but total darkness. Nothing but yourself and the greatest mistake a person could ever make.

"Devon, we have to quit dope. I'm serious, Devon."

"I know you are baby."

"I want to, I HAVE TO, go to Uncle J.R.'s church Sunday," I said. "I need you to be with me."

"I will, Alton. I will follow you to the ends of the earth baby. I love you and I don't want to go through this world without you."

"You promise," I whispered.

"Yes, of course I promise. I love you," she gently said to me.

"I've got to find God again. I can't live like this any longer," I explained.

"What do you want me to do with this dope?" She asked.

I didn't even have to stop and think about it.

"We have to destroy it," I said.

"Okay baby, I'm with you. What do want me to do with it, flush it?"

"No, we have to burn it," I said.

"Why?" She asked.

"I don't know, we just have to."

She helped me off the bed, and we went outside to the porch, threw the sack of dope into our dog's metal water dish, doused the sack with lighter fluid and hit it with a lighter. We cried. Not over the dope, but for us. Until now, we had spent our life looking for pleasure, but we were finally on our way to finding happiness.

I hit rock bottom, but with God's help, I was going to bounce back.

chapter 51

The Change

One of the greatest heartaches for humans is change, especially when you're not prepared for it.

It's one thing to say, "Okay, I need to do things different in my life. It's pretty clear from where I stand right now that the way I have been doing things is not working out to my benefit."

It's a very different story when it is forced upon you.

I was expecting nothing but the worst for both of us. In my mind, I would tell myself that neither Devon nor I wanted to quit dope. We loved it. It was our life. Just give me a few days to get back to myself and I would forget all about this business with God. I was not ready to quit. It had been forced upon us, and quite frankly, neither one of us likes to be told what to do.

I had a thought that maybe God is just too nosey for his own good. If he would just stop looking over my shoulder at what I'm doing we would both be better off. Let's just go back to The Way We Were.

I do what I want. I feel bad later. I pray. You forgive. I do what I want.

But not this time. My heart and soul told me we were going to be doing things God's way this time. I was no longer in charge of my life. His presence was still missing. That Blessed Assurance.

Time and time again in my life, I have collapsed under the pressure of living and given into the sweet call of my addiction. No matter how good I was doing in life, that evil desire of my deadly mistress kept whispering my name. I would just give up and find myself partaking in meth's savage glee and every time, in the end, I would find myself standing in the ashes of all I have worked to build, just to destroy it with my own hands. I had become a phoenix. Build. Destroy. Rebuild.

I would pull myself together, clean myself off, and carry on. Always with God by my side, his presence with me through all I did.

But now I was on my own and I know it. Playtime is over and I was going to have to put some work into finding God.

Things were going to change and it was up to me to make it happen.

chapter 52

New Year's Eve Colwell PDC

I've never made a New Year's resolution in my life, not once. So I ask myself, why not start now? For one simple reason. When I walk out of here in 40 days, I won't be the man I once was, but I plan on being a better man than I've every been.

Not because of this place, at least not directly. I'll be a better man because I'll be walking closer to God than I have in a long time. Truth is, I think I finally appreciate God and the life he had tried to give me. One of the hardest things to do is face the truth about yourself. Truth is, all I want to do is to live out the rest of my life with the minimum amount of suffering as possible. Call me a coward if you want, but the pain and loss as I have suffered at the hands of meth has taken its toll. I want to ride into the sunset with someone who loves me. I want to be a memory, a has been, who truthfully speaking, never really was.

So here's my resolution. The truth. To live it, to breathe it, to spread it, to die for it.

The Truth.

Once you experience life the way I have, at maximum overdrive, through rose colored glasses, in a purple haze, in love, out of love, at the brink of death, you realize one thing. The truth matters. I dare say more than anything else. True to god, true to yourself, true to the ones you love.

A person demands the truth from others, but that, in turn, means that you must also be willing to tell the truth.

Believing in and living the truth gives you the freedom to avoid the pitfalls of life. Embrace the truth and the beauty and simplicity of its pureness and you will find happiness. And possibly, among other things, love. True love. The kind of love that creates those moments of pure bliss. Memories that shine bright as the sun, a blessing from God for your belief in His truth. That kind of love that makes you want to dance in the rain and play in the snow. Embrace the truth and life will embrace you back.

chapter 53

The First Sunday

"I'm nervous Fry daddy," Devon whispered to me as we walked across the parking lot.

"Yeah, I am too," was my response.

"Why are you nervous," she asked.

"I don't know," was the lie I allowed my mouth to speak.

In truth, I knew why I was nervous. I was just afraid to say it out loud. I was scared I wouldn't be able to find God again. I was damaged goods. I didn't even know if God would still want someone like me as His child.

My so-called path to happiness I had been on had been a rough and rocky road. It had left both my mind and soul full of scars left by life's wounds. Wounds that heal slowly. But one thing in my life was now for sure. Something inside of me died that night at Scotty's and I woke with a hunger. A hunger to live again. My craving for meth had been replaced by my need for God.

When a person is in the midst of addiction, nothing matters except for one thing; when was your next shot of dope.

Not only was I destroying my mind and body, now I felt as if I had destroyed my very being. I had sold my soul to the devil to become ruler of my very own meth kingdom. And now, he had come to collect. But I had no intentions whatsoever of just giving up and going back to being ruler of my empire of dirt. I didn't want that anymore. I needed to change. A new lease on life to go with my new outlook on life.

But I couldn't do it along. I knew God was waiting for me somewhere. I just needed help finding him... my uncle, J.R.

"Listen baby," I began, "All we have to do is ease in quietly and head straight for the back pew. Try not to make eye contact with anyone, especially J.R. or Joan, and hopefully, we won't be noticed."

"Dang, Fry," Devon said, "You make it sound like they might eat us for just walking in. Are you sure we should be here?"

"Devon, honey, I have to be here. It's just that uncle J.R. is going to be very surprised to see us here. He's very emotional and makes me the same. He's libel to spot us and point us out to the entire church."

"What?" She said coming to a dead stop.

I'm just letting you know baby."

"Will we have to do anything?" Devon asked quietly.

"No, of course not," I said. "Just sit there and smile at the nice people. They probably won't even notice us walking in."

We walked in during the choir's first song, slithering into the second to last pew, and sat quietly until the singing was over.

"Good morning everyone," J.R. announced as he took the pulpit.

"It's always an honor and a pleasure to be in God's house," he continued amongst a chorus of amens ringing throughout the church. "But this morning is a special morning for me," his voice already beginning to crack from the emotional tidal wave rising in his throat.

"Oh boy," I whispered to Devon.

"Folks," his voice temporarily broken beyond repair, filled with sobs to match the tears that had begun to cascade down his face, "we have a special guest here this morning, my nephew, little Alton and his girlfriend Devon."

All at once we have about 200 eyes staring at us.

"This is a young man who has been a part of my life since his birth. He lived a few houses down from my family until his teenage years." He's a special young man to me and Joan."

And then he began to preach. I mean PREACH. Right at me, or so I thought. Every word spoke of my life and all the trials and tribulations I have put myself through. He never even made direct eye contact with me after he began to preach, but I knew, without a doubt, his words were meant for me. God has laid a message on his heart that could not be ignored. I truly believe that God told J.R. why I was there and how much pain and misery my soul was in. God knew I was looking for Him and he sent J.R. to help me find my way.

Let me explain something to you about southern Baptist ministers. There are two types. The first type is what I like to call the Brian Williams style, also known as "the teacher." Brian is the pastor at my father's church. His family and our family have been friends since the first day he and my father met. It has been an honor to have Brian as a friend in my life. His style of ministering is to teach. He is soft-spoken in the pulpit, does not get excited but knows how to get his point across. You can sit there and listen to him weave his sermon from the Bible to fit into what's happening in your life today and can make you say "wow, I never thought of it like that." Brian is the ultimate laid-back cool dude. He is not afraid to wax about politics or religion or rock and roll. He lives the truth, believes the truth. A true man of God. A prayer warrior with a direct line to the Man himself.

The second type is what I like to call the J.R. Elrod style. J.R., is of course my uncle. He has been a positive influence in my life since I can remember. His style of ministering is to preach. He gets emotional. He likes to walk up and down the aisles. He likes to shout to the heavens. J.R. can bring up emotions you never knew you had. After you hear a sermon from Brian, you feel refreshed and happy. You can go home and discuss his sermon with your family. After a sermon from J.R., you need a nap you're so worn out. His excitement level is so infectious you can't help but to get into the spirit right along with him, which can wear a person out quick.

You don't usually remember a thing he preached on, but you know that it was Manna Sent From Heaven.

If I hadn't been afraid of looking stupid I would have been out there dancing and high-stepping up and down the aisles right along with Uncle J.R..

"Wow," Devin whispered, "does J.R. always get this excited while preaching?"

"Most of the time, yes."

By the time he wore himself down to a hoarse whisper, I was in shambles. I had a grip on the pew in front of us that would have splintered wood with just another inch of pressure. I was so nervous that I was shaking said pew with my G. I. Joe Kung Fu grip so hard that the poor family sitting there was politely glancing back to see what rambunctious little brat was kicking that pew with such zeal that it felt like an earthquake was hitting the church.

J.R. closed his sermon and started the altar call.

"God," I prayed silently to myself, "I want to go, no, I need to go to that alter call. I need to go down on my knees and pray to you like I have never done before."

I'm scared," I said to God.

"I'm embarrassed."

"Please God, give me the courage to let go of this pew and get up and walk down that aisle like a man that loves God, and humble me to bow down in front of all these people and ask you for your forgiveness."

"God?"

"Please God, just a little help to get my feet in gear and moving forward."

And then God answered me. From the third row from the front, my angel appeared. J.R. and Joan's daughter, Tonya, stood up and walked to the end of her pew, stopped and looked at me with a smile that said "I will be your rock to lean on."

"I got to go, Devon."

"Go where baby?"

"To the altar, I have to," I said as I stood up.

I released my grip on the pew in front of us and pulled my way to the end of our pew and made a sharp left towards the front of the church. I hit the altar almost at a dead run and collapsed to my knees in tears, right next to Tonya and then I felt J.R. put his hands on my shoulders and began praying for me. He cried for me. He talked to God for me. He begged and pleaded for me. He reintroduced me to God. When I opened my eyes after J.R. stopped praying for me, I was surprised to find that Tonya was no longer next to me at the altar. She had been replaced by my gift from God...Devon. Her and Tonya were now praying together. Praying for each other, praying for me. Praying for us. I could never have asked for a more beautiful and amazing new beginning to an ugly and almost tragic ending.

chapter 54

New Years Day 1-1-18 Colwell PDC

I know I've started giving you a lot of updates on my current situation here at Colwell. It's just that my release date is getting nearer and a lot of things seem to be happening. Today was a good day. I talked to Mom on the phone for a few minutes this afternoon. She told me that she is now Facebook friends with my very good friend Wanda, who, if you remember, was mentioned in Chapter 4.

She told me that Wanda was coming to pick me up on my release date, what she thought was very sweet of her. What she didn't know was that Wanda and I had already discussed this and she had already agreed to come pick me up and hinted that she would have a surprise with her. At this point in my life, there's only one thing I want as a surprise. DEVON.

I remember the day I picked Devon up from Claxton probation Detention Center, where she had just served a hundred and twenty days. I walked in the front door and immediately spotted her in their release waiting room.

I couldn't hear her because there was a room separating us, but both sides of the room were glass, so I could see in and she could see out. She started jumping up and down, pin wheeling her arms. I swear her tears were so huge that I could see them from where I was standing 50 feet away.

When they finally released her, she came running up to me and threw her arms around me, her sobs uncontrollable. We were complete and whole once again.

My God, how she flooded my soul with joy. The warmth I felt in my chest was like a calming balm washing over my entire body.

A feeling of love.

We ran across the parking lot as fast as we could, afraid they might come out behind us, telling us that they made a mistake and that she wasn't supposed to be released today.

We got in the car and hugged and kissed and Devon put her hand to my face and said "I love you Fry daddy." Just the touch of her hand set my soul on fire. All the way home we talked about things that we would one day try to remember. She laid her head on my shoulder and slept as I drove.

Including her time in Stephens County Jail waiting to go to PDC, she had been gone 8 months. As bad as it pains me and embarrasses me to admit such, I wasn't a faithful husband. I love Devon with all my heart and soul, but I was weak and let the world run my life.

I filled the house with people and drugs so I wouldn't notice she was gone. I visited every Saturday, except for one, when she was in Stephens County, which is about 20 minutes from our house. Her phone account and store account were both kept flushed. She had the nickname "honey bun Queen." The same held true for Claxton, except for the visits, only because it was a four hour drive each way, but I still visited 4 times after I was approved.

Which, all that being said, in no way makes me breaking our wedding vows okay.

I'm sorry Devon. I love you, baby.

And now it's going to be my turn to come home. Right now, all I want to do is walk out of this place with as much of me left that

I can hold on to and run across the parking lot and take Devon in my arms.

There can never be another.

A perfect love changes a person. She's done wrong. I've done wrong. I don't know why we still love each other but I know this; I'm no longer going to look for answers to things that have no answer.

My soul has been battered and bruised enough. I'm not quite sure what causes it more agitation; guilt over my wrongdoings, memories of times I have been done wrong by others, or, just the stress of all of it.

Either way, I'm finished with the hate and anger and revenge. I just want to humbly stumble home with the girl of my dreams.

THAT'S NOT ASKING TOO MUCH, IS IT GOD?

chapter 55

As Water Reflects the Face, so Ones Life Reflects the Heart

I was 24 the first time I did meth. I was lost in grief after my first divorce and was just looking for something to fill the Gap. I didn't like pot, booze wasn't for me.

I became bitter, cursing the life in which I suddenly found myself. I had been a saved Christian since the age of 12, but now, in the most desperate and dark time of my life, I turned to the world instead of turning to my faith.

If I could have only seen the future and the torment that lay in store for me, I would have hit my knees and ask God to hold me through that hurt. Instead, I found myself cradled in the arms of meth. It's pretty easy to tell someone how to save a ship AFTER it has sank. But his time was going to be different. God had jerked a knot in me and got my attention. MY FULL ATTENTION! I had made a promise, a Vow, that Sunday at the altar.

"God, I don't want to die some horrible meth death. I don't want to go to prison. You have sent me a woman who loves me and I love her. Just another chance, God. I'll show you what I got.

I had pushed myself to the brink, over the brink, I guess. Yet god saw fit to bring me back for some reason. Most of my adult life had been a war between Heaven and Hell. The casualties had been great but I was bound and determined not to let mine and Devon's life together become the next casualty of my own personal Armageddon. This time I was going to do things God's way.

"Hey baby," Devon gently said to me.

"Yeah baby," I replied.

"I love you."

"I love you too, Devon, you'll never know just how much."

"I'm so proud of you Alton, you sent everyone away that has come to the house looking for dope. Every person that has called, you have explained nicely that we no longer do that and you invited them to go to church with us. I've seen people tempt you and you're turned them down."

"It's been hard on you too, I know that," I replied.

"You know, I wasn't brought up in church, so I wasn't sure about this whole God thing until we went to J.R.'s church and I heard him preach and I saw how it affected you."

"I want the same for you too, sweetheart.""

2 weeks later, I followed Devon to the altar as she gave her life over to God. We were both growing in our faith. We had picked ourselves up, dusted off, and were just fine without the drugs.

And then, four weeks into our recovery, I got a call.

"Hello," I heard Devon say. "he's right here."

"Oh, hey Pratt," were her last words as she handed me the phone.

Pratt was there from day one. I had known him for about 8 years or more. We had been very close friends at one time. He even slept on my couch for about 3 months during my second marriage while he was homeless. We had done and seen a lot together. As a matter of fact, he even worked for me and my dad at one point. Over the last two years though, we had grown apart. He had drifted off to Florida and had gotten in enough trouble to catch a year in prison down there.

"Pratt, how are you doing?" I said.

"Not good, I need help."

"Ok. Good to hear from you too."

"I'm serious, I need you to come get me right now."

"Where are you Pratt?"

"I'm in the Mexican trailer park in Baldwin."

Not a good place to be and I knew the reason he was there.

"Listen Pratt, I quit meth and I don't want to have anything else to do with it."

"Please, I'm begging you come and get me," he continued. "I don't have anyone else to call. They're going to kill me if you don't get me out of here quick."

"Listen to me brother, I'm done with that life."

"Please Alton," he blurted out, interrupting me before I could finish my thought. "PLEASE."

"Listen, I don't want it around me, do you understand that?"

"Yes, I understand. I won't have anything on me, okay?"

"Second thing," I continued, "where am I taking you?"

"Well, it's kind of late, can't I just stay with you and Devon tonight and tomorrow I'll call my Mom to come get me?"

"Pratt, it ain't like it used to be. I can't have someone living on my couch. I love you like a brother, but you can only stay tonight, okay?"

"Okay," Pratt replied. "Just tonight."

"And another thing," I added. "You have to go to church with me and Devon in the morning."

The phone was silent for what seemed like an eternity.

"I'll be standing up beside the road waiting on you. Hurry up, please," he finally responded.

"Okay, I'm on my way."

chapter 56

PCB

There he stood, right where he said he would be.

"God, help me to be strong, because I'm sure he was probably lying when he said he wouldn't have any dope on him," I prayed to myself as I pulled up to where he stood waiting, ready to jump in my truck.

"Jesus, am I glad to see you," were the first words out of his mouth, his jaw clinched, teeth grinding from an obviously huge intake of meth.

"Hey buddy," I responded. "What are you doing over here?"

"What do you think I'm doing over here?"

"Oh, okay. I see, I see. I haven't seen nor heard from you in almost 2 years, and when I do its to come save you from a drug deal gone bad."

"Sounds about right," he said laughingly. "I'll tell you all about it when we get to your house."

"I can't wait," I said sarcastically.

The next morning, true to his word, he went to church with us. Not only was he like a fish out of water, he was a fish out of water high on meth. He was constantly moving his legs back and forth, turning from side to side, and worst of all, bouncing his legs up and down, which was vibrating the entire pew. I mean from one end of the pew to the other. It was a rough one hour of worship, but nothing compared to the hours that lay ahead for us. We stopped on the way home from church and got us some burgers and fries for lunch.

"So Pratt, after we eat, you gonna call your Mom to come get you, right?" Devon asked, already growing weary of Pratt just the few hours he had been there.

"Yep."

Devon and I looked at each other, neither one liking the sound of this. We got home, ate our food and I told Pratt that me and Devon were going to be outside finishing our garden project while he made his phone call. Ten minutes later I told Devon to go inside to get us a couple of glasses of water, but while in there be sure to listen to what was being said in Pratt's conversation. Ten minutes later she comes out without the glasses of water but was carrying a heavy dose of anger by the look on her face.

"Okay, Fry daddy, so here's the deal."

"Calm down, baby," I said.

"Ohhhhh no, I'm gonna to have to calm you down after you hear this."

"Let's have it."

"Okay, well, first of all, he was just sitting there on the couch, doing nothing. So after I fixed us some water I just asked him what was up. He said nothing. So I asked him when was his Mom coming to get him."

"Okay."

"Okay? Okay" Nothing about this is okay," she fumed at me.

"Well, tell me then, what is it, Devon?"

"His Mom told him to forget about it. She didn't care where he was at or where he wanted to go. She wasn't going to pick him up or give him any money to get anywhere."

"What?" was all I could choke out.

"He's not even allowed to visit her house, much less live there. He's been lying the entire time about having somewhere to go."

"Yep, that sound about like Pratt," I said. "I guess all we have to do now is find out where he wants us to drop him off cuz he ain't staying here."

"One step ahead of you, baby," Devon replied with a smile.

"Okay, so where do I have to take him?"

"His grandfather's house."

"Okay, that's no big deal. His Grandpa just lives down in Stone Mountain."

"Uhhhhh, just a tad bit more bad news there, Fry."

"What now?"

"His Grandmother doesn't want him down there either."

"And," I said.

"No and, there's a "but" but no and," she said with a look that was halfway between amusement and total rage.

"But," she continued, "his grandfather said that he could use their other home."

"Where's that at?" I asked.

"Panama City Beach."

"Florida?" I said gasping for air.

"Yes, Fry, Florida."

I felt like I had just took another throat punch from God. Devon and I were just getting on our feet, both spiritually speaking and financially speaking, and I get this bomb from my past dropped right in my lap.

"Wanna know the best part?" Devon asked me.

"Oh goody, it gets better?"

"He has a pocket full of dope."

I don't need this temptation, God, I told myself. I knew he couldn't stay any longer cuz he would be just like a cockroach that burrowed in on the couch and we would never get rid of him. Before you knew it we would be right back on the dope again. We would never get rid of him.

"What are you going to do, honey?" Devon inquired of me.

"Let's go," I replied.

"Go where?"

"Pack a bag honey, we're going to Florida."

chapter 57

Let's Ride

"Well honey, as much as I would like a vacation to the beach, I think we have a bigger issue to address."

"What's that, Devon?"

"What are we going to drive?"

"My truck, of course."

"Your truck?" she questioned me.

"Yes, Devon, my truck."

"Your 20 year old truck, with 240,000 miles, that gets 13 miles to the gallon?"

"One in the same," I replied proudly.

"The same one that has no brake lights or backup lights, right Fry?"

"We're on our mission from God, Devon. Nothing can go wrong."

"We are not the Blues Brothers, and plenty can go wrong," Devon said to me.

"Look at it this way, baby," as I continued. "If we take him to Florida, we will probably never seem him again. Odds are, he'll be out of our lives forever."

"I'll be ready to go in 30 minutes," she said amused.

So, let's just recap all of the things we had going against us. First, we had a drug addict on a couch who had no intentions of going anywhere, except to his grandfather's condo in Panama City Beach, Florida. Second, he didn't have a red cent to his name. NOTHING...so it would be completely up to me to fund our little field trip. Gas, food, cigarettes for all three of us. Third, my truck was literally a piece of junk. No one in their right mind would consider driving it that far. And even if we did make it there and back it would cost me a heck of a lot of money just in gas. Money we didn't have to waste. If all that wasn't enough to stop someone with just a smidgen of common sense dead in their tracks, this last one would. Fouth, A HURRICANE.

Yes, a bona fide hurricane that was predicted to downgrade to a tropical storm by the time it made landfall. But, nonetheless, a hurricane.

Pratt told us that his grandfather was already down there fishing, and that he would be waiting on us to get there. An hour later we were loaded up and heading down the road to Panama City Beach, Florida. We arrived at 5 a.m. Monday morning. Of course, no one was there.

"Pratt, where's your grandfather at?" I asked, with a serious chill in my voice.

"Georgia."

"Pratt, did your grandfather tell you that you can come down here and stay?"

"Nope," he replied matter-of-factly.

"So what were your intentions here buddy, to break in your grandfather's condo and hide out till you get caught?"

"Naa man, I'm not breaking in. I know where he keeps the key."

Devon and I waited in the truck, not wanting to partake of any felonies that were being committed. After 5 minutes of sitting there, we saw a light come on and Pratt stepped out onto the balcony and motioned for us to come in.

147

"Not a good idea, Alton," Devon hissed at me.

"Yeah, you're probably right, baby. But I'm dead tired from that drive. Let's just go and rest for a little while, okay?"

"Okay," Devon said.

We sat down on the couch and I went out like a light. 2 hours later I woke up to gale force winds beating the trees outside into submission.

"Devon, wake up baby, it's time to go."

I found Pratt passed out in one of the bedrooms. I didn't bother to wake him. I walked back into the living room, and found Devon. She was smoking a cigarette and looking out the sliding glass doors at the impending wrath of God heading our way.

"So much for a day at the beach," she said with a hint of disappointment.

"We got time, we can drive over to the strip, check out the ocean and then go see a few tourist shops if you'd like."

"If you feel like it baby?"

"I don't mind one bit, purdygurl."

"What about Pratt?"

"What about Pratt?" I asked.

"Are we just going to leave?"

"No, I guess not."

"I walked over to the house phone and found a pen and piece of paper to write on.

"Pratt, here's twenty bucks. I'm going back home. Good luck."

"That's nice of you to leave him a twenty," Devon said.

"I don't have a ten," I replied.

We left, and despite the wind, spent the morning and part of the afternoon stopping at every shop that caught our eye. Then it got dark. VERY DARK. Then the rain started.

"Honey, I think it's time to go," I said.

"I think you're right."

As it turns out we were just a little too late. We were forced to drive about 50 miles an hour all the way back to Atlanta due to heavy rain. Oh yeah, I forgot about the other little problem with my truck. My windshield wipers only worked when they wanted to. Sometimes they would work for 10 minutes and then quit for 20 minutes. Other times they would work for an hour and quit for 10. It was hell on the highway. There were times when we had to pull over and wait for them to come back on. I felt like Gilligan. Our three hour tour was turning into a shipwreck nightmare. I felt like we were never going to make it home. As a matter of fact, we didn't

"Devon, honey, call your Mama and Daddy and tell them we're going to come by and spend the night with them. I can't drive any further until this rain quits. I am wore out."

"Good idea. I know you got to be tired baby. That was one heck of a driving job there."

I wouldn't want to do it again, I'll tell you that."

"I love you, Alton Fry," she whispered in my ear as we pulled in to her parent's yard.

"Devon, I love you too."

Final tally: $190 for gas, $60 for food, $20 for Pratt, $60 spent shopping, $20 for cigs, $15 for oil. $365 total cost, plus I missed work on Monday and Tuesday. A small price to pay for peace and sobriety.

Pratt, on the other hand, didn't fare so well. Three weeks later he was arrested for grand Theft auto and spent the next year and a half in prison. It's been 14 years since the day we left him sleeping in his grandfather's condo, and I still have yet to see or hear from him again.

Hope you're doing okay, buddy.

chapter 58

Calvo

Besides getting rid of Pratt, and clearing the first real hurdle placed in our path, another important thing happened on our way home.

Devon and I talked.

We talked about our plans for the future. We talked about how proud were of each other. We talked about our families and the changes that they had seen in us. Yet, for all of our talking, there was one big question that remained. What to do with all this newfound time on our hands.

In steps my Grandfather, Calvo Fry, one of the greatest fishermen the state of Georgia has ever seen. This man was an expert about everything fish. Where to go, when to go, what kind of bait to use, bank or boat. It didn't matter. This man knew his business.

He had been retired from the state for about 20 years, and in that time he had amassed a collection of rods and reels into the hundreds, along with at least a dozen tackle boxes, fully stocked, for all different types of fish and their locations.

The man was a freaking fishing genius. I don't know whatever led me and Devon to decide that we wanted to take up fishing, but there we were, standing with my statuesque grandfather, in the middle of his very own miniature Bass Pro Shop, being quizzed about what kind of fishing we had in mind.

"Well, PawPaw, we haven't really thought that far ahead yet. We just want to catch something big,"

"Sounds like you're looking for catfish," he responded, with a grin full of wisdom, a half smile that would brighten up any cloudy day.

"I got just what you're looking for right over here."

"We'll get both of you two poles each and a tackle box."

"Thank you, PawPaw," Devon and I both said.

"I got a question for you,' I said to him as we were loading up our expensive gear that my precious grandfather had just gifted us. "What kind of bait should we use?"

Simple question, right? Simple answer, right? An hour later we were as well versed as two rank amateurs could be. We knew what bait to use, where, and at what time. We were in fish info overload.

But that was my grandfather for you. A kind, gentle, giant of a man. He had a heart of gold. Two years later, Devon and I were on the river the day he died. I can't help but think that he was smiling that half smile in heaven when he looked down and saw us enjoying ourselves on a beautiful summer day, like he had done so many times in his life.

GIVE A MAN A FISH, FEED EM FOR A DAY. TEACH A MAN TO FISH...THANK YOU PAW PAW.

chapter 59

Where to Go

I had not been fishing in years, and Devon, growing up in the city, had never been. Now don't go thinking to yourself that fishing is simple; all you do is put a worm on a hook and drop it in the water. NOPE. You have to know how to tie your hook so the fish don't just pull it off. You have to know how to cast your line so you can place it with precision, and yes, of course know how to bait your hook, which in itself is a science. Do it wrong and the fish will just jerk it off, or, as Devon learned on the first day of fishing, if you don't put it on good enough, when you cast you will watch your line going in one direction and your bait in another.

We decided our first fishing trip would be to a 3-acre lake owned by a family friend located about 5 minutes from our house. Long story short, after 3 hours of fishing the score was me 4, Devon 0. We were having a good day just sitting there on the banks of this lake. It was peaceful here. The day was beautiful. The sky was beautiful. The lake was beautiful But most of all, Devon was beautiful. God was an artist and this landscape was his canvas. But his most precious piece, was of course, my soon to be wife.

The sun was going down behind the trees, leaving only fingers of daylight peeking through the branches. The heat of the day slowly turned into the dark cool of the night. We had discovered a calmness that we had seldom known in the past, but we were quickly becoming aware of just how much God's serenity and peace we were beginning to enjoy in our once troubled lives.

I've been a lot of places in this world, and seen a lot of amazing things, but nothing can bring a smile to my face more than thinking about the days that we just sat on a dock and just laughed and giggled at each other. Nothing in the world but the two of us. We were no longer flying high on drugs; we were flying high on our love. Yeah, I know that may sound stupid and corny, but we lived it. It was very real.

"You bout ready to go baby?" I asked her casually.

"No."

"No?'

"That's what I said, no,. I'm not ready to go," she replied without ever taking her eyes off her pole.

"Well, it's starting to get dark, baby. How long you plan on staying?"

"As long as it takes."

"As long as what takes," I inquired.

"As long as it takes me to catch a fish. We're not going anywhere until I catch a fish," so mad she was almost in tears.

And so began our new addiction, which in the site of God and our families, was a blessing of epic proportions. Up until this point in our lives together, we had been living in chaos, a meth fueled race towards destruction. And now we were spending our time killing worms, instead of ourselves.

We had made our families believe that we had given each other a suicide pact, sealed with our blood, by the way we have been acting and living up until this point. We didn't believe in going to bed mad. We just stayed up all night and fought. We didn't believe in beating other people up. We just beat ourselves up. We didn't think.

We just did. We didn't like to think because thinking wakened pain, pain from both our pasts before each other. We were both scarred from life's little ups and downs that we had fumbled and crawled through before we met each other. I think we clicked so well because I understood her pain just as much as she understood mine. Meth became the friend that helped us to kill the pain of the wrongs perpetrated in our histories. Plus, it was the lubricant that helped us to turn a blind eye to misdeeds we allowed each other. Or so we told ourselves.

But in reality, the meth was nothing more than the true cause of most of our pain. Dope, of any kind, is a coping mechanism. It helps you to cope with the lies you tell. It helps you to cope with the pain you caused. It helps you to cope with life's disappointments.

Funny, now that I'm not on drugs and have been locked up for 9 months, those so-called disappointments don't seem so disappointing at all.

God, how I wish I could go fishing.

chapter 60

Changes

Three things happened in our life around this time.

First, we got married. It was a warm October afternoon at the little church on top of Okey Mountain. The trees were alive with the color of autumn. the white paint of the old church shined like it was only a day old. The air was thick with excitement from our family and friends who were joined together to see these two wild spirits tame one another.

My God, was she ever beautiful when she walked through those front doors. Every single person in the building was in awe of this beautiful, golden-haired princess, who was hand-in-hand with her father. I'll tell you this; when she walked through those two doors, God walked into the room right behind her, with a smile on his face.

She was an absolute vision of beauty. Her long blonde hair curled down past her shoulders, her blue eyes shone like diamonds. Looking at her standing there in the same dress her mother had worn some 20 years before, I felt like a complete man.

I know I was a lucky man because I was getting to marry my best friend.

When I heard her say yes, I think that may have been some of the most powerfuls words I had ever heard. I looked into those blue eyes and I knew that I had finally found the woman God made for me. There were no second thoughts, no confusion in our heads or hearts that day. We were in love and everyone knew it. I love you, Devon.

The second thing to happen in our lives, was, as you read earlier in the book, was that we finally went to court on our drug charges.

I took the felony charges, Devon took the misdemeanor chage so she can continue school. We both used our first offender status. She wound up with 12 months probation and $1,000 fine. I received 5 years probation, six months house arrest with monitoring and a $3,000 fine.

And the last thing to happen in our lives was that we discovered Habersham Mills.

Habersham Mills was a cotton mill that was founded in the early 1900s by the Stribling family. But, it was more than your average cotton mill. It became a village. They built dozens of houses around the plant, so many in fact that they also built a schoolhouse and baseball field for that community. In order to meet all the water demand, they dammed up the Soque River and created Habersham Mills Lake. They later built another dam, further down the river and also additional plant buildings by the river between the two dams. This is where my grandparents, Reynolds and Laura Mae Elrod lived and started their family. It is where my mother and father first lived after they got married.

During this time, The Village grew to a bustling little community with it's own cafe and post office. I'm proud to say that my mother was the postmaster for over 30 years. and then, one day, it was all gone. The plant was sold to a Fortune 500 company who promptly closed it down. The people moved away. The houses were left abandoned and eventually torn down. It was turned into a ghost town. All except my Mom at her post office. She went to work everyday and waited on customers who were long gone, never to return. Eventually the giant, faceless corporation decided to auction off all the property and lots along with the main plant and lower buildings.

What I'm trying to do here is just give you an idea of what the place looked like, ok?

Picture this. A 100-acre lake, about 2 miles of river water and no one around except for my sweet Mama, Ruth.

It was time for me and Devon to go fishing.

chapter 61

After Midnight Colwell PDC

I can't sleep. I feel it growing, getting stronger day by day, night after night. My civil wars once again raging a full fledged, bloody battle. It's me against me.

It's 2:30 a.m. and I'm so confused and torn I can't sleep. I toss, I turn, I talk to God, I pray to God. I cry out for God's peace. And still, no peace do I find.

The battle rages on with no end in sight. I feel that I will never find the sacred comfort I seek so desperately until I surrender to the cold arms of death. I'm scared. I'm angry. I'm worried. Part of me can't wait to get out of here so I can be with my family once again. To step up and be the man that takes over the burden, MY BURDEN, that I have left my parents to bare.

The other part of me wants to stay here in this unreal world of childhood and hide. I don't have to work. No bills to pay. someone does my laundry for me. I have free cable TV, free food, free medical care, everything is free; EXCEPT MY FREEDOM. This place is an all-inclusive resort, without the five star rating. They won't let you check out.

I'm scared I won't be man enough to make it in the real world again. What if I'm such a screw-up this is where I'm meant to be: I feel like a frightened little child who buries himself under the covers because you're scared a monster is under the bed, and a blanket is all it takes to ward off the boogeyman.

I want to do the same. What's worse, I keep asking myself the same, tangled up question; what do I deserve? The world or prison? At this point, I have to ponder, is there even really a difference.

I don't know what to do.

Dear God, I just want to scream. I want to stop feeling. Stop hurting.

Being locked up has taught me that I have more than death to fear. In fact, death is the least of my worries. It would actually be a problem solver. What does worry me though, is being 47 years old and staring over with nothing. It is the fuel that feeds my worry.

I feel a strong sense of both helplessness and uselessness, both running my soul ragged and leaving me with an awful emptiness. I never felt this way about myself until now, and so, I have to pause and ask myself, is this my cross to bear?

Is this karma, making the world right?

This question, although posed by myself, only acts to further flame my anger and hatred. I'm angry for letting the world get the best of me. I was the smart guy, the go to guy, the guy with the money and beautiful girl by my side. You were supposed to be my oyster. Instead, my stubborn anger turned me into the world's roll of toilet tissue.

Most people's anger is only skin deep. Mine, on the other hand, runs to the bone. I know it will cripple me in the end. It's working it's venom through my body as I write, poisoning all the good thoughts I am creating with God. Undermining all the promises God has laid out for me.

If I will only allow His will to be done.

"God, I'm trying. Sweet Jesus, you know I'm trying my best."

It's nights like these that test my faith. I beg God to help me, to get all these insane thoughts away from me. But I can't even finish a prayer because I started attacking myself with nonsense. The battle for my mind rages on.

"Dear God," I begin to pray.

"Shut up, look over here," the voices in my head counter.

"I can't do this without your help, Lord," I continue.

"He's busy, pal, call back later," they snicker.

And on, and on, and on...

I just want to be normal.

"Please God, help me."

I don't want to be angry. I don't want to be full of so much hatred that it burns my soul and everything I touch. I just want to be Alton. Just plain old me. I want to make my parents proud of me one last time before they pass away. See the love in their eyes and a smile on their face, knowing I was man enough to stand up and do the hard thing, the right thing, and face the world head-on. LIKE MY DADDY DID. AND HIS DADDY BEFORE HIM. Take this anger and hatred from me and turn it into courage and hope. I've learned God, ohhh how I have learned from my mistakes. I surrender. I give up, God. Please end this civil war and reunite my mind, my body, my soul, my spirit into one. While there's still something good left in me. I pray that one day this pain will help, if not myself, someone else.

chapter 62

Thanks Mom

"Hey Mom," I said as Devon and I walked into the post office to visit her.

"Hey babes. What are y'all doing?"

"Oh, nothing much," I continued, "we were thinking about going fishin'."

"Where y'all going to?"

"Well, we was hoping to try to fish down here somewhere. I've always heard stories about people catching big fish down here."

"Oh yeah, I've see some big fish that's been caught behind the main plant there, and quite a few from the lower plant also," my Mom told us.

"Well, seeing how it's all been auctioned off to people who aren't local, I don't reckon they'll mind if we fish a little, would they?"

"You can do what you want, but if you ever get caught, you better not get me in trouble too."

"We won't," Devon and I replied in unison.

And so began the great Habersham Mills Fishing Adventure. Let me give you just a few examples here, if you don't mind.

We started taking Taylor, my daughter, fishing with us and I had been teaching her how to bait and cast. This was her first trip to Habersham Mills with us, which had very little clearance to cast due to trees. I was trying to do it for her, but she, like her father, is bull-headed.

"Tay," Devon began, "just let your Daddy cast it the first few times to show you how not to get it hung up in the trees."

"I can do it," Taylor replied.

And back and forth the three of us went, until finally, I just gave in.

"Go ahead baby," I relented.

The kid put everything she had into it. A little too much, actually. We're using some very expensive rod and reels that had come from my grandfather's inventory. She let go with her first cast, and well, she let go. OF THE ENTIRE ROD. It landed in the middle of the river, about 25 feet away from the bank where we were standing.

"Daddy, Daddy, get my pole," Taylor yelled at me.

"Why, in God's name, did you do that for?" I yelled back.

"I didn't mean toooo," as her tears started.

"What are you crying about," I asked, holding back my own tears. "I'm going to have to tell Papa Fry you just threw $150 to the bottom of the river.

"I wanted to fish," Taylor continued, "and now I don't have a pole. I want your pole Daddy."

"What," I yelled.

"Giver her your pole, Fry," Devon chimed in.

"What am I gonna use?"

"Just sit down and be quite and enjoy watching your two favorite girls fish," Devon said in her best 'you better listen to me voice.'.

Now I really wanted to cry. I wanted to fish, dammit.

"Thank you Daddy," as she realized her and Devon had won out.

"Oh, and one other thing, Daddy."

"What is it now, Taylor?"

"PawPaw Fry really loves me. I'm his favorite great granddaughter," she continued, "so me and Devon have decided that you should go ahead and tell him that it was you who lost his pole."

"You do, do you?"

"Yes, Fry, we do," Devon said matter of factly.

"Two against one, I guess I don't have much choice, do I?"

"We love you," Devon replied.

"Yeah, Daddy, we love you," Taylor said right in unison with Devon.

"Yeah, girls, I love you too.

chapter 63

The Mill PT 1

We fell in love with fishing at Habersham Mills. Actually, we fell in love with fishing in general. During the summers, we were fishing probably 5 days a week with a lot of that time being spent behind the old Cotton Mill, down by the river. We never knew what was going to happen when we hit the riverbank.

One time we were sitting there when the fish we had on a stringer started pulling away from the bank. We only had five or six fish on the stringer and we both thought it's kind of odd that these fish had suddenly mustered up enough strength to plan an escape.

"Pull em up and let's see what's going on," I said to Devon.

All I heard was a scream of death that had me running over to Devon to defend her from some unseen attacker.

"What are you screaming about, baby?"

"It's eating our fish."

"What's eating our fish?"

"Pull em back up and see for yourself," she replied.

As I bent down to pull up the stringer, I remember thinking to myself what a big baby Devon was for letting, what I assumed to be a large mud turtle, scare her. NOTE, NO MUD TURTLE. Instead, what I found was a 4 foot long water moccasin that had decided to feast on one of our fish and had swallowed said fish completely. We had some pretty nice fish on that stringer, but the snake wasn't giving up and I wasn't about to fight with him about it. Devon was standing 10 feet away from me and still yelling about getting that snake away from her. I didn't want it around me anymore than she did. I pulled the stringer out of the ground and watched him float away with what had to be the feast of his life.

Another time, we decided to take our beloved Jon boat, yet another gift from my grandfather, out for it's first spin on the river. Probably would have been a good idea for a first trip on the water to have been during daylight. But, oh no, we couldn't wait. We put in about halfway between the upper plant and the lower plant, and I started rowing upstream toward our destination. The bottom of the dam. It was kind of creepy and sexy at the same time. On this beautiful water with my girl, nothing but the glow of our lantern to keep us company. That was really the only sexy part there was. The creepy part was all the trees hanging over the banks, creating complete and utter darkness that surrounding us beyond our lantern.

"Hey babe," Devon began, "you think this is a good idea?"

"Well, now that you mention it, probably not."

"It's spooky out here," Devon said. "Maybe we..."

And that, my friends, was the end of our conversation because we were under attack. What sounded like a shotgun blast landed at such close range to us that it splashed water on Devon, who promptly began screaming and shoved the lantern into my face, which almost caught my hair on fire.

"Get that lantern out of my face, Devon, are you crazy?"

"Get us out of here now, Fry," she screamed, the lantern still only inches away from my face.

"You just blinded me, woman. I can't see which way to go. Get than damn lantern away from my face right now," I screamed back.

"I'm not doing anything till you find out what's going on around here," she continued in her high scream pitch. That same "oh God, save me voice from the snake incident.

"Devon, calm down," I said, very much trying to hide the absolute terror that had also engulfed me.

After a few moments of paddling to the silent sounds of banjo music playing, I realized exactly what had happened.

"Listen, baby, that was nothing more than a beaver we just happened into and it slapped it's tail in the water."

"After a moment of pondering this, she asked, "and just how do you know it was a beaver?"

"I'm a man. We know these things."

"Paddle faster Fry. Get me back to the truck now."

We are on the way baby, we are on the way.

chapter 64

The Mill PT 2

"Hey Devo," which, by the way is not a typo, it's just another nickname I have for Devon, "you want to go fishing?"

"Are you serious, it's snowing outside?" she said laughingly. "Do fish even bit when it's this cold?"

"If they're hungry enough," I said.

"Load up big boy, I'm ready whenever you are."

And so we headed down to the mill to fish in November, in the middle of a snow storm. We went to our favorite spot, which just so happened to be at the bottom of a steep drop off about 200 feet long that leveled out at the bottom into flatland, perfect for fishing.

Before we go any further with this tall fish tale, I need to give you some background info to give you a better idea of what's going on.

Like I told you earlier, the mill and all the property, around 900 acres, had been sold in a huge auction. People came from all around the world to attend the auction and bought land. A lot of these people cleared off their lots, cut roads down to the river and then just never did anything else with it. There wasn't a single house being built on any lot. It was a literal ghost town.

Mama eventually got permission for us to fish behind the plant from the gentleman who had purchased it, but we took it upon ourselves to broaden our horizons, so to speak.

What I'm trying to tell you is that we just went wherever the heck we wanted to go to fish.

We stopped at the top of the muddy hill, pondered whether to do a normal drive down, which required a 4 wheel drive on a good day to come back up, or just get out and walk down or just say the heck with it all and head back home.

"Honey," Devon started, "you think we will be able to get back out if we drive down?"

"Are you questioning my driving ability or my truck," I snorted, ready to defend both me and my truck, like a real country boy would.

Let me stop our story right here for a minute to give you women a little life lesson. THERE IS NO CORRECT ANSWER TO THAT QUESTION!! You should never, EVER, question a country boy's driving abilities or how tough our four-wheel drive trucks are. We will tear up a $40,000 truck with a quickness to prove a point. It doesn't matter how dumb the challenge is, or how obvious failure is, cuz we will take on all comers, as Little Miss City girl Devon was about to find out.

"Baby, you da man, I know that, and your truck has gotten us out of more tough places than I can remember, but that's a steep hill and it's nasty outside, plus your tires are almost bald."

She should have never made a comment about my tires being "bald." There's nothing wrong with being bald. Baldness is something that is inherited from your mother's side of the family. Wait a minute, we were talking about tires, right?"

"Well Devon, we need to drive down or we could carry down all our poles and tackle box and drinks and snacks." Which, by the way, was also essential equipment for trips. "Or we can just go on back home if you don't think we can get down and back up."

"Go for it, big boy."

"I thought so," I said proudly, as I started to ease down the hill.

You know what, let's have a moment of realness here. I've never admitted this before, and I'm embarrassed to now, but by the time I slid around the curve at the bottom of the hill I knew there was no way we would ever make it out. But I wasn't about to ruin a good day of fishing by sharing such useless information with Devon.

After about an hour of fishing, we had answered our own question. No, fish do not bit in the middle of a snowstorm, except this one really dumb fish that Devon caught that must have just accidentally ran into her hook and got caught.

One hour, one fish and we were freezing our butts off.

"Hey baby," Devon finally piped, "I'm ready to get warm, how about you?"

"Yeah, I guess so. Don't look like we're going to catch anything today anyway."

We loaded up our things, jumped in the truck, turned the heater on full blast and started back up the hill.

"Hey purdygurl,"

"Yes, baby."

"I sure do love you," which was my attempt at building some good will that I knew I was about to need.

"I love you too, Alton," she said. "I don't care if we didn't catch any fish but one today. I just love us being together like this."

Little did she know we were about to spend a lot of time together.

"Well, I'm glad to hear that. I love our lives together now, too. The drugs are well behind us. All the fussing and fighting is behind us. I got my best friend back."

"It's always going to be me and you, right, Fry daddy?"

"Devon, you are the one God made for me. I could never be happy without you."

"God, I love you," she whispered in my ear as she kissed my cheek.

"I'm really, really glad to hear that you love me so much," I said, "because you are probably going to be very mad at me."

"Fry, are we stuck?"

"Baby, we ain't going nowhere."

chapter 65

One Fish

"I told you, I told you, I told you," Devon's loving chit chat now replaced with loving scorn.

"No, you didn't. You told me to go on."

"Don't blame this on me Fry. You're the country boy, you should have known better."

"Yeah, I should have known better than to listen to you," I said proudly.

"Listen here, buddy boy, best thing you can do is just shut up and figure us a way up out of here."

"Give me your phone and I'll call someone to come pull us out."

"I didn't bring my phone," Devon said. "Where's yours?"

"I didn't bring mine either," I whimpered.

"What are we going to do, Alton?"

"Well, Devon, looks like I ain't got but one choice."

WALK.

"Well, Fry," she yelled, "and just where are you going to walk to? There's no houses around for miles."

"Well then, I need to get started before the snow gets any worse," I said.

"We're a team Fry daddy. If you're walking, I'm walking."

And so we begin our snowy journey back to civilization in search of help. From were we were at, it's around a mile, mostly uphill mind you, back to Habersham Mills Road, the main highway. By the time we got there we were really cold, we were really tired and we were no longer talking to each other. That was the easy part of our journey. Once we hit the road we had a choice, go right and hit the closest house about a mile away or go left and hit the closest house about a half a mile away. A half-mile walk up a 45 degree snow-covered side of a mountain. It's not really a mountain but it is a heck of a hill. Just ask anybody who knows. We stood and stood and stood.

Being the president and CEO of this company, I made the decision that we will head left up the hill. She cussed me and cussed and cussed me some more. I took it like a man.

It's going to be okay baby. My buddy Scott's uncle lives at the top of the hill. He'll let us in to use the phone to call Amanda."

"Amanda?" Devon, yelling once again. "Your 17 year old niece, Amanda?"

"Yes, that Amanda."

"Just what is your 17 year old niece going to be able to do for us?"

"Well, for one thing, her Jeep is a 4-wheel drive. I'll call her to come get us and to take us back to my truck, get my tow strap, hook to her Jeep and she can pull us out."

"She'll never go for that, Fry."

"Sure she will," I said as we began out climb.

Let me tell you a little something I learned that day while climbing that hill in the middle of a snowstorm with a woman by my side. The people of Habersham County ain't what they used to be!!!!!

When I was a kid, I remember going places with my Dad and every car we met he would raise his hand and get a wave back. Whether you knew them or not. People would smile. They would wave, they would stop and ask if you needed help if you even looked like something might be wrong.

That was then. This is now.

On a good day, no one in their right mind would be walking up the hill on Habersham Mills Road. On a good day, I'm telling you. And yet, here we are, in the middle of a snowstorm, two people, one of them being a stunningly beautiful woman, walking up this hill. You can see the look of stress on both our faces, and yet three cars passed us by, without even a slight tap of their brakes. I actually think that two of the SOB's sped up a little so as not to have to make eye contact with us.

"Wow, Fry daddy, what happened to that famous southern hospitality?"

"Must be Atlanta transplants," I mumbled under my breath.

"What was that?" Devon asked.

"Nothing honey."

We finally made it to Scott's uncle's house, Mr. Bill Free. We explained the situation to him and he let us use the phone to call Amanda. I explained the situation to her and she said she would be on her way.

"Thank you Mr. Bill for letting us use the phone," I said.

"No problem son, but tell me something."

"Yes sir."

"What in the world made you think it was a good idea to go fishing in a snowstorm in the first place?"

"Well, Mr. Free, I'll tell," I began. "My wife is from Atlanta and she don't know any better. I tried to tell her fish don't bit when it's this cold, but she just wouldn't quit nagging me until we went fishing. Why heck, as a matter of fact, it's her fault we got stuck."

"Well I'll declare."

"Yes sir, let me tell you," my courage beginning to build while Devon was in the kitchen with Mrs. Free. "I told her and told her it was a bad idea to drive down to the river, but she just kept on and on about my truck being junk. She even told me I should just shut up and man up and put the 4 wheel drive to good use."

"Well I'll declare," he repeated again.

"What was a man to do?" I said in my best broken man voice.

"Boy, when a man get pushed like that, they liable to do all sorts of nonsense,' Mr. Free said.

"Exactly," I replied, as Devon walked up behind me.

"Hey honey, what are y'all taking about?"

"The weather," we both replied in unison.

"Well, Mr. Free, I appreciate you letting us use the phone. We're going to step out on the porch and smoke and wait on my niece to come get us."

"Thank you very much," Devon added.

"Yaw welcome."

We stepped out to the front porch, lit a cigarette, took about two drags and here comes MY DAD pulling up.

"I told you Amanda wasn't going to go for this, Fry."

"Whatever," I said, as we got into the truck, knowing I didn't have the energy to fuss with Devon because I was sure I was about to get a good father to son talking that would be requiring all my attention.

"What in the world were you thinking," my Dad started in. "Fish don't bite when it's this cold."

"Hungry ones do," Me and Devon said at the same time, causing both of us to just burst out laugh

My Dad wasn't amused.

"And just how many fish were hungry," he asked.

"Just one," I replied.

I was a little upset with my niece for busting us out to my Dad, instead of coming to help us like I asked, which, in hindsight, was a blessing seeing how the next day turned out for us.

chapter 66

It Ain't Mine

We went home and decided on a plan of action. First off, we came to the conclusion that Amanda's Jeep would not be able to pull us out. We also realized that we had no friends with four-wheel drives to come help us, so we were left with only one option. A four-wheel drive tow truck.

We called around to get prices and found out that only one company had such a truck, hence, the outrageous price they were asking for a simple tow job. We agreed to meet at the plant at 10 the next morning and they would follow us the rest of the way to our truck. Okay, here's how things went. The guy pulls to the top of the hill, releases his front winch and walks down the hundred feet to my truck and hooks it up. He starts winching, using a hand held remote. My truck winches his truck DOWN the hill about 10 feet before he realizes what's happening. He stops and gets in his truck and tries to just pull me out, by backing up. NOPE. He spend the next 10 minutes just mutilating the ground spinning his tires. He finally stopped and decided that he would put slack in the winch cable so he could back up past the destroyed ground to try and get a better grip. NOPE. He backs up and starts again, now not only is he winching me but he's also trying to pull me with the truck. I mean this dude is sliding 50 feet from the left to the right, just plowing this property up. Ten minutes doing this and he has once again allowed his truck to be pulled back down to the top of the hill where he started in the first place.

His next plan of action is to back up to the road, put his rear winch around a tree, drive towards me till he has no rear cable left, then run the front winch all the way out toward my truck and any shortage he may have with the front wench cable would be made up with two 100 foot chains he had.

GREAT IDEA, RIGHT? Backup to clean ground so you get better grip, then tie yourself off to a tree.

So we unhook my truck, he backs up. Ohhh, wait a minute, he's TRYING to backup but can't seem to get any traction due to the fact that he just laid waste to our exit. Yes, the four wheel drive tow truck is now stuck. Everyone involved in this fiasco is now in a state of shock and confusion. Devon is mumbling something about idiots fishing in the snow. The tow truck driver is cussing up a storm to someone on the phone. And I'm about to go into total meltdown, trying to add up in my mind just how much this one fish is now going to cost me.

An hour later, the calvary arrives in the form of the tow truck company's owner, in his $70,000 pimped out personal truck. He pulls halfway across the field, but remains on somewhat level ground. He turns around so his front is facing the trees. He wraps his front wench around a tree and backs down to the tow truck. They use the chains to hook to each other and then he starts wenching. And winching, and winching, and winching, until... he drains the battery dead on his truck. No, I'm not lying. I'm not exaggerating the truth even a little. This is how it happened.

He had to take the battery out of the tow truck, then hook it up in his truck to crank it. He unhooks the tow truck battery, hooks the battery back up to the running truck to let it charge and then puts the good battery back in the tow truck. Thirty minutes later in a lot more torn-up ground, he finally has the tow truck sitting on level ground next to his truck. Using both truck winches and about 5 miles of logging chains, they had pulled me up the hill and across the property, which now looked like a military battle had taken place on it.

"Mr. Fry, I'm sure sorry about the mess we made to your land here," the tow truck owners said to me. "Did y'all buy this at the auction?"

"It ain't my property."

"Oh, who does it belong to?" he inquired.

"I don't have a clue."

"You ain't got permission to be here?"

"Nope, shore don't, so I suggest we get to moving, How much do I own you fellows?"

"Mr Fry, if I had known this was not your property, I would never have done this job."

"Hey, I don't blame you buddy, I wouldn't have either."

"I'm going to need you to pay in cash because I don't want this mess to ever be able to be tracked back to my company."

"I got'cha dawg. I was never here either," I chuckled. "So how much I owe ya?"

"Four hundred."

My chuckle just went to a full-blown, hysterical laugh.

"You kidding, right?"

"No sir, not at all. 3 hours for the tow truck, plus two hours from my truck."

There was no debating this. There was no talking it over. He wanted FOUR HUNDRED DOLLARS!!!

"I don't have but $370 on me."

"That will do sir. Just let me have it so we can get out of here."

"Well, can I keep like $5 so I can get some gas on my way home?"

"No sir, you cannot."

"Thank you, have a good day, and never call us again."

"Oh, by the way, how many fish did you happen to catch?"

"Just one hungry one."

chapter 67

Devon

Hey baby,

It's been a long time, huh? Around 5 months, I think, since the last time I saw you. You were sitting in the courtroom I hope to never see again in my life. You were about three rows back from the front with tears in your eyes. Every time we would look at each other we were both saying silent "I love you" to each other. It's been hard these last 10 months locked away from the world. I don't know how people do this for years at a time. I don't know why they would want to. I miss talking to you. I miss being able to touch your face as you sleep on my chest. Your safe place you used to call it. If you could have only found a better man than me to watch over you, to love you, I wonder how different your life would be.

There are some nights I lie here awake, thinking of the love we once had. A love so deep that I know when I step out of here it will still be there.

As the Bible says, "love forgives."

You remember when you came home from PDC? There were days and nights you couldn't stop crying. You would just bury you tears and anger in my chest and I would hold you, just hold you, till

177

all your fears had passed. I wonder, will I do the same? Will you do the same for me? I wonder, is time no longer on my side. Have these last 10 months given you a new lease on life that doesn't include me?

I am now the hapless, pathetic, ex-husband who does the daily check on Facebook to get updates on what's happening in your life? A soul damned by its own desire to have what cannot possibly be his? Or will I be the one living life with you?

Sometimes I wish I could just forget you. I wish I could stop loving you. Just forget that we ever existed. I cannot. God didn't build me that way, remember? I stand and fight. Don't run. I don't know what's next for us, but I do know this; when God has finished painting our lives, it will be beautiful. It will be us holding hands, smiling. In love. Happy once again.

I love you, Devon.

chapter 68

A Big Deal

God was blessing us. Now that I look back as I'm writing this right now, I finally realize how God was purely blessing us. Smiling down on the transformation taking place in our lives. We were staying off drugs. Mine and Dad's masonry business was booming. Devon had graduated from college and had a great job she really loved and the fishing was still great.

No, there is no "but" here in our story. Our lives were as perfect as you could ask for. We were doing things most people only get to dream about. We went to Mexico, to the Maya Riviera, which is about 2 hours south of Cancun. We swam in underwater caves there, we rode four wheelers through a jungle, we walked halfway up a mountain and climbed into a crystal clear river that came out of the mouth of a cave and we floated down it until it dumped into the ocean. Beautiful doesn't begin to describe the things we saw there.

Everyday we woke up in love, wondering what the world held for us that day. Most importantly, we were still in church, giving thanks and taking care of the gift God had given us. Our lives had become amazing. Full of mystery and wonder. Now that I look back, it blows my mind to see all the miracles that bloomed in our lives.

That day, years before, when my spirit died from the trash fever, I was reaping what I had sowed. God gave me a brief taste of hell. I didn't like it. For the second time in my life, I felt like I was reaping what I had sowed. Only this time, God was looking down on us in approval. I was learning that life happens, just the way it happens.

We were clad in perfect happiness and as we learned, happiness is a choice. I felt like we were in an alternate universe. Living on another planet, we had come so far from where we once were.

We went to Walt Disney World twice, one of my masonry customers thought so much of me and Devon that she asked us to go on both occasions. Not only did she buy us passes to all four parks, EVERYDAY, but she also bought almost every meal we ate, AND gave us both $100 per day to spend as we saw fit.

One Thursday evening we were sitting at home, bored, just watching TV. The show was something about the monuments in Washington that interested the both of us. We looked at each other, smiled and started packing. We drove all through the night and into the next morning until we found ourselves sleeping at a rest stop just outside of the nation's capital.

"Hey baby," I said, as I awoke with a smile.

"Hey pookie," Devon replied.

"You ready to make history?"

She smiled that beautiful smile and said, "You know I am."

We had come up with a plan in the middle of the night to conquer the entire East Coast, anything that was famous, we wanted to see it, do it, or taste it. Whatever it may be.

We started our day in Washington D.C. We visited every monument or museum we found interesting. We got back to our car late afternoon and headed for Philadelphia, Pennsylvania to get ourselves a Philly cheesesteak. We got there and found ourselves a motel, one without hourly rates and rested for about an hour. I went to the office and got all the tourist brochures they had at the front desk and we decided on a restaurant that was billed as having "the best cheese steak in Philly." "Whatever". I've had better cheesesteaks from Subway.

We left Philly and headed towards the ocean at Atlantic City. We learned several things about the Garden State along the way. First, a person could go broke paying tolls on the interstates. You can't drive 5 miles without hitting a tollbooth, and they dang sure ain't spending the money on the roads, cuz they sucked. Second, their nickname should be changed from garden State to "junk cars abandoned on the side of the road state." Our goal for New Jersey was to hit Atlantic City and walk "Under the Boardwalk, down by the sea."

We got there, but after a quick inspection of "Under the Boardwalk," we decided to stay on top of the boardwalk. Atlantic City, quite honestly, is really a rundown dump, and of course, while we were there, we visited Trump Casino.

I think I'll just save myself a trip the next time and stick with Harrah's Cherokee Casino.

Next on the list was the one and only New York, New York. We started driving and didn't stop till we got there. Well actually, we landed in Newark, New Jersey at the Holland Tunnel Lodge, which is only a ten minute subway ride to the city. You can't afford to stay in New York, unless you're just big money.

"We need a room for the night," I said, trying my best to mask my southern twang.

"Will that be the gentleman's special?" the desk clerk inquired.

"Well, I don't know, what is the gentleman's special?" I asked.

With a perfect straight face, she looks and me and replied, "The gentleman's special is our two hour rate, sir."

"Oh," I said.

"Ohhhhh," I repeated with a grin. "No, I actually need a room for the night."

"Did you just call me a prostitute?" Devon chimed in after a few moments of pondering.

"Oh, no m'am. I wasn't implying anything. I just..."

"Really?" Devon interrupted, "cuz that's what it sounded like to me."

By the time she had calmed down we had gotten $30 off our bill. Good job, purdygurl.

The next day we took the subway to the world famous Grand Central Station and started our adventure in the city that never sleeps. We ate pizza that was so big you had to fold it in half, just like what you see on TV. Again, whatever. I'll take Pizza Hut any day of the week, as far as that goes. I don't care if I was in Italy, I would still find myself a Pizza Hut. I love you Pizza Hut. Feel free to use me in a commercial. I'll work for free pizza. This is how deep my love for Pizza Hut is; Domino's is an 8 minute drive from my house. If I don't want to leave my house, they'll even deliver it to me if I so desired. Pizza Hut is a 20 minute drive each way and they don't deliver. Sorry, Domino's. That 20 minute drive there just helps me to build my appetite and the 20 minute drive back is just long enough for me to eat three slices. Four, if I drive slow.

I'm sorry, where was I at? Oh yeah, New York City.

We had one of the famous hot dogs you get from street vendors. The ones you always see in the movies. The kind that you just walk up to the cart and they fix the dog for you. These things were freaky in color, in taste and smell. Attention citizens of New York City, you are all invited to my house where I will grill you a hot dog like you've never tasted. Or we could just go to The Varsity.

We stayed for 2 days, and I have to tell you this. If you ever get a chance to go to New York City, don't pass it up, you won't regret it.

And so, after checking out of the "whore motel," and leaving one of the most amazing cities on the planet, we made quick stops in York, Hershey, and Gettysburg Pennsylvania.

The incredible trips, the good jobs with the good money were great, but they took a back seat to the most important thing in our lives. We had finally found peace and joy. Taking unnecessary risks, such as meth, no longer appealed to me. We were now grabbing everything God offered us and were making sure that we praised Him and gave Him thanks for all.

As I sit on my bunk writing this, I feel so stupid after reading back over what my life once was. I lost my self-esteem, my friends and almost my life.

I am a perfect imperfection. Truly one of God's own.

chapter 69

METH

I guess it's time to address the 800-pound gorilla in the room. METH.

I'm going to give you probably the most honest talk about meth you will ever hear. Some words will be facts, some just feelings. I don't know how you're going to feel about it, or how you're supposed to feel about it. All I'm doing is giving you a stark, inside glimpse to the thoughts of a meth addict.

Doing a shot of meth is like getting hit by a bolt of lightning. Your body becomes electrified with excitement, makes you feel young again. It feels like you discovered the Fountain of Youth in a needle. You got energy that knows no boundaries. Your mind opens up to ideas that you would other wise never imagine. It makes you feel sexy. It makes you want sex. It is power. It is money. Pre-meth is like living your life without having tapped into you five senses. But now, this little clear shard somehow not only fine tunes your five senses, it helps you to discover five more you didn't know existed. It makes you feel close to heaven. That's day 1. Day 2, maybe 3, meth begins to show it's real face. Day 4, meth finally reveals it's true identity. THE DEVIL. All of a sudden, the fun is gone. All those good feelings and bright ideas are missing. You quickly learn that meth creates just to destroy.

Meth is a jealous mistress. She will make sure that you have no one else in your life but her. It causes paranoia on a level that cannot be measured in fathoms. It will embrace your being, setting off a war between you and the shadow people. You hear tortured voices that bring you to your knees, causing you to ring your hands and cry out for them to show themselves. But no one shows up, for this battle is purely in your mind. It leaves you begging for divine intervention to help fill the loneliness of this one man battle that has now rubbed your mind raw.

It is said that hell has different levels with many chambers on each level. I believe the perversion of meth will be in every room. What would be more sickening than to be tortured 24 hours a day. You want to sleep, you just want to rest but Satan says no, here's more meth. You beg for just a drop of water, but instead, you get just more meth. But hey, that first day was a blast. I had fun. I think?

You lie to yourself trying to find that first day again. Just a bigger shot will get me there. Or, maybe I should try smoking or eating it. Hey, there's an idea. I'll just eat a little bit of dope while I'm fixing my shot of dope and then I'll just smoke me some dope in between my shots. You know, just to help me maintain.

You soon realize that you can't live without the meth or the lies. The meth, because you're now hooked and the lies because they are now the lubricant that allows your life to function with the smoothness of a German luxury sedan.

You murder sleep, day after day, night after night, you laugh in the face of rest. All the while, the evil presence grows stronger, while you grow weaker. You walk around with a melancholy that clings to you like your shadow, a foulness that becomes a constant reminder of your wounded spirit. It leaves you in tatters, almost like you're being devoured. And then the first signs of death appear. It's you eyes. The twinkle is gone, that sparkle that makes them the windows to your soul, now only reaveals an inner calm that has gone missing and a moral landscape that is about a s deep as a thimble.

You become ignorant to choice. You learn quickly that in your new lifestyle there is but one choice and it leaves you no room to hesitate.

More dope. More dope. More dope. In between your shots of death you catch flashes of something that once might have been. A hope. A dream. A life worth living. Something that reminds you of you when you still had a life.

It truly is a sickness, a cancer that grows inside of you like a demon that knows no restraint, only vicious greed. I can't go back to meth again. I can't. I know I will die. I escaped one last time from her, but I don't have it in me for another battle with my longtime companion. God, I'm going to let you fight this one for me.

chapter 70

Good News or Bad News

Devon and I were heading on three years clean and sober. We had finally reached middle-class America. We were living in my little bachelor pad I had built after my divorce from Taylor's mom. It was an 800 square foot room that was suitable for a single man, but not the type of home a beautiful woman deserves.

And so, we decided to build our Dream Home.

Mine and Daddy's masonry business was still booming so I decided the smart thing to do was to start buying lumber every time I got a check and would store it in our masonry warehouse where we kept our equipment and materials. We bought lumber, windows, doors, anything we could find that was on sale, for three years. At night I would draw the plans for our house and then we would go over them till we had them the way we wanted them. Every time I would work on someone's home, I would see something new and unique I wanted to do on our house, so I would go home and draw different house plan that included my new, brilliant ideas that I had stole from other people's house plans. It was a work in progress. And then one day we said the heck with this. It's now or never. Let's get started. The only problem was that our new 2000 square foot home was going to set smack dab on top of my bachelor pad, which we were still living in. Luckily my Uncle J.R. has a mobile home he was willing to rent us. We packed all our clothes and a few dishes and moved in. Everything else we put in storage. It took about three days to get moved out and back in over at J.R.'s and Joan's. On the fourth day, we met back up with Daddy at the house. He had sledgehammers, chainsaws and shovels ready for us. And so we started the demolition on our little home that had serviced us so well.

At lunch break all we had gotten done so far was about ten sheets of tin removed and one corner of the house cut through with the chainsaw. My Dad was pouring sweat. Devon is passed out underneath a tree from heat exhaustion. I can't believe just how well I build this little home.

"Son," my Dad began.

"Yeah, Daddy?"

"This is taking way too long, we need to try a different approach."

"What you got in mind?" I inquired.

"Let me see that can of diesel."

Me and my Dad both love fire, we love burning stuff, so why not burn the house down.

"Want me to call and get a burn permit before we start?" Devon asked.

"Nah, we'll keep it small," I replied.

"Yeah, you're probably right. Be kind of hard explaining that we're going to burn our house down," Devon said.

At the end of what I would call a VERY successful day, we had burnt one house to the ground, had put out four brush fires, destroyed only one acre of pasture and didn't have but a dozen or so trees burnt or singed. Not bad for a day's work.

Me and Daddy took the next 3 moths off from work and put everything we had into getting the house done. I had some really great contractors that I work for that were there to answer any questions I had about building.

Harold Welborn, who was a lifelong friend of my Dad's, and one of the builders we contracted from, was a wealth of information and help. He and I had the nickname little buddy for each other. If not for my little buddy, I would have never been able to start my house, much less finish it. Harold loved life and lived it to it's fullest. I miss you little buddy.

With the help of Devon's parents and a few of our friends, we moved in four months later. It was an incredible task that could not have been accomplished without our families, and of course God. Once again, we were reaping the harvest of our hard work and worship of God.

I remember Devon crying the first night in our brand new bedroom. She had her own house. More than a house, it was a home. Our home, built with love.

On the front porch we sat two white rocking chairs. There was nothing special about these two chairs except that they were ours, and to us, they represented our future. They were where we would sit at night and look at the stars and know that's how many days we would be together. Those two old rocking chairs is where we would sit during the day and watch the sunset over Alec Mountain and know that this where we would spend our final days. On our front porch, smiling back on the life we had lived and the love we had shared. We were still drug free, had built a new home and we were madly in love. That was the good news. The back news was that Devon had a headache.

chapter 71

Bad News

We took Devon to the hospital for her headache, it was that bad. They put us in a room and we waited an hour for the doctor to come in and tell us she had a migraine. He sent us home with a prescription of Lortabs for her pain.

This was the beginning of the end. Let me tell you something right now that I know to be a fact because I have lived through it.

I believe in my heart that meth is the devil; at least a form of the devil. I also know this; when the devil wants to get high, he pops pills. That's how bad they are. I know that for a fact because I lived through what they turned Devon into.

Meth blurs the lines of reality, but pills refuse to even acknowledge there is a reality. They darken a person's soul, creating an abyss. Once again in our lives we were facing life-altering change.

After we finished our house, my Dad retired from the masonry business. I ran it for the next two years with tremendous success, still just blowing and going.

And so were Devon's headaches. She might go a month without a headache, but then we would be at the hospital twice a week for the next three months with her migraines. And then she finally found herself a pill mill.

A doctor who does nothing but prescribe pill after pill. You just tell him whats wrong and drop a hint or two about what works best for you and tah dah, you got yourself a couple hundred pills every month.

You want to see a person go insane. Give them a taste of something they like and then try to take it away from them. Sex, drugs, money, gambling, even religion create a hunger and then try to starve them of it and you have created a monster. Your very own Frankenstein.

If that wasn't enough trouble, I turn on the TV one day to find out that the last ten years of incredible growth in the United States was all just some sham, created through mortgage lending. North Georgia was hit hard by the mortgage crisis. To say that we were hit hard is like saying Hurricane Katrina was nothing more than a heavy rain to New Orleans. We had bankers going to prison, we had builders going to prison, we had building supply companies going out of business. No joke. All three of those very things happened right here in Habersham County.

I was working on the old Hall County Jail doing a remodeling job for one of my general contractors when construction in North Georgia came to a screeching halt. The old jail had been bought by a company called CCA, Corrections Corporation of America. They were turning the building into a holding facility for ICE; Immigration Customs Enforcement.

THE FEDS...I finished all of the masonry work that was to be done to the building and then went to work with the general contractor as the assistant job foreman to help him finish out the job. That was our first financial blow.

I went from making $1200 a week, sometimes much more, depending on how long and how hard I wanted to work, all the way down to $600 a week. That's a serious cramp in lifestyle. And still had to contend with Devon's headaches.

She became known as a pill seeker and visited all the surrounding medical facilities. Every time the same thing. Nothing wrong with you but a migraine. Here's some pills, now go home.

Back at work, we were about a month away from completion. CCA decided that in order to get to "know" the newest addition to the family of the 66 prisons they already ran across the country, they insisted the two gentlemen who were going to be the warden and the assistant warden should be on site for the final phase of the remodeling.

Long story short, after spending several weeks together with these gentlemen, they offered me a job.

Yes, me, the former drug dealer, was now going to go to work at a Federal Detention Center as a corrections officer.

Which was going to be a super shock to my system, but I saw no other choice but to take the job. This would be the first time in my life that I actually had a 9 to 5 job. Taxes. Health Insurance. 401k. Dental Insurance. Paid days off. Paid vacation. Up until this point in my life I never knew there was such a thing as a paid day off or paid vacation. We went to work and got paid or we stayed home and didn't get paid. I like the sound of all these, what's known in the real world as "benefits."

I did mention the health insurance? Which as it turns out, is some pretty expensive stuff, but as it also turns out, is a good thing to have.

chapter 72

Que Vadis

I had been working at CCA for about 3 months at this time. I think it was around the first of 2010. I was outside on a smoke break and decided I would check my phone. I had a text from Devon telling me she wouldn't be home when I got there. She was leaving me. As a matter of fact, she was already at her parent's house with her belongings. 50 miles separated us but at that moment I felt her hand explode through my chest, grab my heart and squeeze until it shattered.

Once again, our train has derailed.

So I did what every other man who falls in love with a beautiful woman does. I was going to fight for what I love. If I failed, so be it, I would endure. I quickly learned I was no match for her addiction. I became exhausted chasing after her like a starving child chasing after a meal, no less hungry for her attention and affection than a child looking for life-sustaining sustenance. She wasn't coming back. It was up to me to find peace with what had happened. I was depressed and angry. I became bitter and was uncertain if I would survive. Once again, darkness engulfed me. We finally filed for divorce.

Everyone says it takes time to get over such things. Does that make time my enemy or my friend? I heard that saying so many times from so many different people, I just wanted to scream, a scream so powerful and full of rage that it seemed our house would tremble.

I really had no idea what to do. So I just gave up.

My life became unacceptable, a Greek tragedy full of meaningless days and nights. I became too tired to care, too defeated to go on fighting. All I wanted was to find a poetic end to my misery. I awoke from my Camelot to visualize the world as it really was, a barren wasteland built on lies and deceit.

I was living a mirage, heading for something I needed to live only to get there to find it had all been a cruel joke my mind conjured up. We didn't even speak anymore. Devon had become a black hole of emotion. Empty. A void. Morality became a far away planet that couldn't be reached from where she was living. It was a luxury she neither wanted nor could afford. Her lies were her gift of the galaxy and she gave with ease. And yet, in spite of my deeply warring emotions, I couldn't stop loving her. But she no longer loved me.

Sometimes when the truth becomes too clear, a persons sorrow and sadness become more weight than they can carry. It becomes impossible to get up and walk away from. Instead, you embrace the crushing weight of your life with a gleeful madness. You ask yourself, was I better off living the lies that allowed me to continue on with our unordinary life, able to breath? Or was it the side effects of my constant denial of what lay in from of me the very thing that wrecked us and destroyed our false harmony?

It was Sunday morning, two weeks before our court date for divorce. I was laying in bed, Eyes Wide Shut. My heart wounded with the sickness no healer could cure. My mind and soul in competition with each other to see who could cause me the most pain.

In all honesty, I'll have to admit I was feeling quite sorry for myself. I was thinking about how not to think when I heard my front door open and close gently.

194

My Mom always cooks Sunday lunch, so I just assumed it was either her or Daddy bring me something to eat, and, of course, to check up on me. I sensed movement in my bedroom door, so I rolled over to say hey and let them know that I was just tired from a double shift at work.

It was Devon.

She was standing in the doorway, staring at me, with tears rolling down her cheeks.

I'm at a loss for words to describe this moment.

Soulful, maybe?

I felt like I had just walked into a whisper with nothing else left to say. A faraway breeze that reminds you of a beautiful memory.

We stared at each other. Her tears becoming sobs. Even through her emotional state, I was still amazed at her beauty and couldn't imagine why she was with me in the first place, much less why she would come back. But I also had that feeling of a dog that had been beaten and wounded a little too much. I was still wary of her uncaring and cunning persona that she had shown me the last 9 months. I feel like she made it her mission to put me through more pain and misery any man this side of hell has ever known.

I was hurting, my life was a shambles. I felt so alone. I was alone. She was still just standing there, neither one of us saying a word or moving. She was a goddess in distress, a deer caught in headlights. And so, I did the only thing that came to my mind. I pulled the sheets down and slid over. She got in next to me on her side of the bed that for the last 9 months I had slept on. My futile attempt at keeping her close to me, my grasp at turning nothing into something.

We embraced and I wiped the tears from both our eyes. She laid her head on my chest, her safe place, she called it and we never spoke a word. We didn't need to.

chapter 73

Really Bad News

We were okay. Well, we were working on being okay. That's the good news. But...

You've known by now there was going to be a "but". One time in our entire story has then been no "but", but since then, our lives have been nothing but one but after another. There were five buts just in this paragraph alone. Six if you count the one in the last sentence. Anyways...

Devon had been home about 3 months now, and her headaches hadn't gotten any better. We were at the ER in Gainesville, Georgia when the doctor came back with the news. She has a brain tumor. Yeah, that's some pretty bad news. Good news is that she had a job with insurance. Bad news is she just got fired. More good news is I had my job insurance. Really bad news is that when we separated I took her off of my insurance. So the really, really big question was, would my insurance consider her tumor a pre-exisiting condition? Which as anyone who's ever dealt with an insurance company will tell you, is a no-go- for coverage. I didn't care. I had to try. I had to do something. The thought of losing Devon terrified me. All my hopes and dreams centered around us.

Me and Devon, not me and some replacement, not someone trying to be her and take her place with me. NOT SOMEONE I HAD TO PRETEND TO LOVE.

Her condition was known as a pseudo cerebra tumor. It wasn't an actual tumor on her brain, but rather her spinal fluid was clogging up at the base of the brain, causing it to swell, which was the cause of her migraines. This was putting so much pressure on her eyes that she was starting to lose her vision. Without a permanent stent placed in her brain and tubing that ran to her kidneys so she could pee the excessive spinal fluid out, there was only one thing that could be done at the ER to ease her pain. Spinal taps.

My company was having open enrollment for insurance in March so we blindly scheduled her surgery for the last week in March, hoping beyond hope and praying to God that my insurance would accept her.

Her last spinal tap had left her a bloody mess. The doctor missed, the baby nurse tried and missed. Finally we had to wait for the baby doctor to get there and it took him two tries to finally get it in. Normal pressure for spinal fluid is 17. Devon's topped out that night at 41. She was sitting on the edge of the bed as they were draining it. She was exhausted from the trauma.

"You okay, purdygurl?" I asked as I wiped tears from her eyes.

"No."

"Be strong baby, they're almost finished," not able to hide my own tears.

I'm so sick of this," she began, "I can't do this any longer," she whispered in a hoarse voice.

"Devon, I love you, and you will be okay. Do you understand me? I am nothing without you."

"I need you to be strong for me," I said through tears of emotional pain.

"I can't be."

"You can, and you will."

"I love you Pookie."

"I love you too, Devon."

The first week of March came and I turned in all the necessary paperwork to the human resources lady. The next week I got my new insurance card, none of which had Devon's name on them. As it turns out, she was left off my insurance cuz the HR lady said I didn't turn in a copy of our marriage license.

I went numb. How was I going to tell Devon that she's going to die cuz I left out a piece of paper. Her warrior. Her defender. Her knight in shining armor who would lay down my life for hers and you're telling me I didn't turn in a piece of paper?

You're wrong, wrong, wrong. I argued up and down that they never asked me for our marriage license, that this was the most important moment in my life. I didn't forget no damn piece of paper lady, you're lying to me. You never asked me for no marriage license. Her answer; sorry, better luck next time.

Let me tell you something about myself. I am very good at turning easy into difficult. If my years in meth had taught me one thing, it was not only how to survive, but thrive, in chaos. You want to fight with me HR lady? You're about to get one you'll never forget.

And so began my quest for redemption. CCA is a company that runs 66 prisons nationwide. They have over 15,000 employees. They stretch all the way from Nevada to Puerto Rico. They have contracts with US Marshals, ICE, federal, state and local governments. They have lots of money and lots of lawyers. I did not care. I got on the company internet and found the president of the company's email address. I got my boss's computer and began to write and I didn't stop until I was sure I got my point across.

I just let him know that my fishing buddy was in trouble, that this truly was a life-or-death situation. It was a letter of love. I wrote about my best friend, the woman I couldn't do without. Sorry, I can't give you the details. That was my love letter to Devon. It belongs to us. And just to make sure that he knew I was serious, I sent it to about 10 other people with a title that sounded important. Little did I know that one of the titles wasn't just a person, but rather a position at all 67 facilities. It went to every single prison they ran. My warden about fired me for not telling him what I was doing. He came to work the next morning and was blindsided with HUNDREDS of emails from people at other facilities wanting to know our story. Frankly, my dear, I didn't give a damn whether he like it or not. I WAS A WARRIOR IN BEAST MODE AND I WASN'T GOING TO STOP UNTIL I SAVED MY PRINCESS.

Two days later, they reopened the insurance enrollment for 48 hours for anyone in the company that may have also had the same problem that I had. I won. I WON!! I went up against a company worth hundreds of millions of dollars and I won.

Still have any questions about how deep my love for Devon is? I have not even began to understand the depth of the human heart, nor will I ever understand how it works. But I do know this, there's nothing more satisfying, exciting, beautiful and terrifying at the same time than to bathe in the bliss of having someone to love, and being loved back. In my opinion, it's a walk with God.

chapter 74

Deja Vue

Devon survived, and was just as beautiful with no hair as she was with her Goldilocks in flow. Although her health was back to normal, our lives were far from it. I'm not going to dog Devon out to make myself look good, nor will I lie about what happened just to make her look good. The truth is, our lives spun so far out of control this would be a 1000 page novel if I were to try and tell you everything that needs to be told.

Maybe you've heard of the movie, also a book series titled "Lemony Snicket's Series of Unfortunate Events." It's about 3 siblings whose parents died, then their house burns down. After that, they're kidnapped, separated, tortured and locked in cages. Basically, anything that could happen to this family happened.

Well, they ain't got nothing on the Fry family. I'm going to give you the highlights, or maybe I should say the low lights of our lives that led up to the great crash of 2015.

Buckle up and hold on. And once again, remember, this is nonfiction. I'm not making any of this up. Simply put, we had a wave of internal weakness. Yet again, I had the opportunity to run to God to be my rock and shelter and once again I embraced the world.

I started going to the same pill mill that Devon was going to. It was my dumb, stupid, misguided attempt to try and keep up with her addiction. She was eventually arrested for prescription fraud. The day of her court case, she left me once again. She came back eventually.

When she returned we started going to the clubs in Atlanta. The kind of places that most Americans only think exist in movies. I was getting Adipex from the quack doctor, which is methamphetamine in pill form. That wasn't going to work for me. We started with the legal prescription pills, Adipex. That Adipex lead to cocaine. Cocaine lead to...drum roll please... my dear old friend meth.

Five years clean down the drain.

Our emotional grip on life quickly evaporated. Insane things are done in the name of love. Love will cause a sane man to kill, a peaceful man to wage war. Through the ages of time, love has willed many a man to destroy, not only others, but also themselves, both mentally and physically. Many a man has learned the hard way that love is a high price to pay to live.

I am no different. Five, six months later she left again. This time it was for a guy who told her she was pretty and taught her how to shoplift at Walmart.

I was still working at CCA and doing meth. Okay, time for a truth moment. My meth addiction is huge. Beyond huge. There's no way I could afford to buy my own meth, but that's the whole secret to drugs. You get someone else to pay for your sack. Buy low, sell high to cover the cost of your own addiction. When you buy in bulk, it's cheap. For example; you by the quarter pound you have around $10-$12 in a gram. You sell grams for $70.

So to answer your question, I'm sure your asking. Yes, not only was I doing drugs, but I was also selling drugs while working in a federal Detention Center. Not to the inmates, mind you. Everyday I worked around a dozen Federal Ice agents. They thought so much of me that they asked me to join their fantasy football league. I DID. No joke. I was living dual lives. I was a functioning addict.

Everyday was a test to see which way my moral compass was pointing. I still had principles I would die for, yet at the same time there were lines that I had no problem crossing.

Most of the time I just walked around in a mindless rage at the thought of Devon once again being MIA. She eventually came back with her new job skill; shoplifting. I eventually fell in also. Yes, I should have known better. Congratulations for being the one millionth person to tell me so. When it comes to love there's only one thing you need to know. Common sense and heartbreak are seldom on the same page. In fact, they're not even in the same area code.

They usually avoid each other at all cost. Heartbreak is a bottle of bleach and common sense is your favorite red shirt that your dead grandma gave you. One splash of heartbreak and you can throw common sense in the trash can.

Devon gets caught in Anderson, South Carolina shoplifting a $9 shirt while I was in another store actually shopping. I come outside to see her surrounded by half a dozen cops. We were in a borrowed car that had a half ounce of meth in it. My meth. Someone else's car. Devon and the police are all around the car.

So, I just kept walking all the way down to the other end of the strip mall and then I walked straight out to a field covered with three foot high grass. I hit my stomach and started crawling Rambo style across this overgrown field trying to get away from the cops.

It took me two hours to move 1200 feet to a Hardee's. I went inside and threw away $400 in gift cards I had in my billfold that we had made that day returning stolen items because I was so freaked out that I would get arrested and have all those cards and have to explain why I had them.

I called a cab. He came and took me to a motel at the state line, where I was sure I would die. I lived.

I was missing for 3 days, along with my very dear friends car. Which, by the way, I was sure I saw being towed away as I did my Rambo crawl. As it turns out, it was still setting right there in the parking lot a week later when her Mom took me up there to get it.

I was sure it was a trap. I made her Mom cruise the parking lot for ten minutes and then park and set for ten minutes, while I got up my nerve to go get the car. I was so freaked out, high and paranoid that I about had her Mom in tears begging me to get out of her car so she could get back to Georgia.

Charges against me for grand theft auto were dropped the next day and Devon was released 15 days later. Yes, as a matter of fact, our lives were falling apart. If you think it sounds crazy now, you should have seen it in living color.

Months pass and once again we separated. Then she wants to come back home. This time I said no, because my parents were sooo happy she was gone and wanted us to stay that way. But of course I couldn't stay away from her. And so we did what any normal, loving couple high on meth would do. We hid her car down the road behind the church. I would pick her up every afternoon and take her home with me and then every morning I would take her back to her car and she would go on her way.

Well, one night I took her to Walmart in Toccoa. I go do a return on some dog food and while I'm waiting in line she walks up behind me and tells me to hurry up. I ask why and she explained to me that she just stole an $800 all-in-one computer and its sitting in the backseat of my car.

Here's another truth-telling moment. I could come up the road with a pound of meth in my car and not think one thing in the world about it but when it comes to shoplifting, a stick of gum would send me into a nervous breakdown, and here she is telling me she was walking out with one of the most expensive items they have and is now telling me that she wants to go back and get a TV.

HELL NO.

I told her I'd have no part of it, that I'm going to the car and she needs to come right along with me. In one ear and out the other. So she walks off to get her TV and I walked off to the car. She walks out with a flat screen TV. Only problem is she's being followed by loss prevention. They stop her, she runs, not away mind you, like most shoplifters, BUT STRAIGHT TO MY CAR.

She jumped in and we take off, a very big fight on the way home, but we make it home and so I'm thinking cool, we made it out alive. But that would be the last time we ever do that.

2 Days later, Toccoa Police Department calls me at WORK...

I use my charm and wit to squash my involvement. I let a person I know borrow my car. Can't believe he would do such a thing. The female? Gosh, I have no clue. Musta been some dope whore. The investigators seem to believe my responses and tell me they don't have any other questions on this matter.

Next week, I'm called to the front desk. I get to the entrance (I was outside) and realize that I still have a quarter ounce of dope and needles in my pocket. I can't go in because I have to walk through a metal detector and then go through a pat down. So, I casually walk over to the outside garbage cans and tossed my little black bag inside.

Once inside, I realize I am being arrested by the Toccoa Police Department for felony theft by taking. They knew it was me driving and they knew who Devon was. My Warden, assistant Warden and Chief of Security were not happy.

I was handcuffed on the spot. I was stripped of my ID badge, my keys and by the time I hit the door I had lost my federal clearance that took me a year and a half to get.

What they didn't know was that Devon had taken me to work that morning, so at the time of my arrest she was in the employee parking lot taking herself a nap after a long morning of shoplifting.

10 p.m. that night my best friend at the time shows up at Stephens County Jail to bond me out.

"Thanks brother," I said as we walked across the parking lot.

"What are you going to do now," he asked.

I took the driver's seat and he sat in the passenger seat.

"We're going to go get my dope."

"Hey baby," someone whispers from the empty back seat.

"What the," was all I got out.

"Oh yeah, I forgot to tell you Devon is hiding in the trunk of your car," my buddy replied.

"She has warrants too for the same thing so we thought it would be best for her to hide so as not to be spotted."

"Good thinking, baby girl."

"Thank you baby," she said over the roar of the road. "Could you pull over now and let me out? I'm dying back here?"

"Sure thing," I said as I slammed the gas pedal to the floor as we hit a section of s-curves posted 25 miles per hour. Just a little payback for me losing my job.

No harm, no foul I thought to myself as I began to giggle at her yells to pull over.

We made it to Gainesville and I parked four blocks away from CCA. I put on a hoodie I had in the car and walked the four blocks down to the front door. My plan was to walk right up to the front door of the building and start going through the trash. I was going to act like one of the numerous homeless people that came out at night and walked around the front of the building going to the cigarette ashtrays looking for butts. I got right to the trash can when one of my former co-workers stepped out for a smoke break. I turned and quickly walked away before they realized who I was. I ran back to the car to tell them what had happened.

They decided they would give it a try. I drove down the street and about twenty feet before the parking lot entrance, they jumped out and walked up as I parked across the street just a block below the exit of the parking lot. I didn't even have time to put the car in park, before I saw them running down the street carrying the entire garbage bag they had just stolen out of the front of the Federal Detention Center.

Yes, we were crazy. Just another side effect of meth.

I popped the trunk and they threw the bag in, slammed it shut and jumped in the car as I start to drive away. We drove straight home and dumped the bag on the front porch so we could search for my black bag. We found it, went inside and shot dope the rest of the night.

I said goodbye to my old self that night. The one who had tried to maintain a lifestyle of normalcy, one with a respectable job, and I said hello, once again, to the wisdom of the world.

chapter 75

Winner Takes Nothing

Our journey from salvation back to sin didn't take very long. It was a short and winding road. I wonder if I would even ever find my way back home again.

It was a journey that quite often left me miserable, standing with clenched fists, cursing the world and cursing myself for my apparent stupidity.

I was taking the human adventure, which is quickly turning out to be more powerful and alluring than anything my limited mind could imagine. We were about to take our little traveling meth show worldwide. No joke. We went to court on the shoplifting charges. They couldn't prove that I stole anything, which I didn't, so I pled guilty to obstruction for lying to the investigators. I got one year misdemeanor probation. Devon plead guilty to the shoplifting charges and was sentenced to two years felony probation. She finally quit leaving me. But once again, she got caught shoplifting. This time a $6 pack of batteries from the world's largest hardware store.

You wanna know just how stupid meth heads can really be? Here is a million-dollar example. The Loss Prevention officers at the store waited for us to walk out at the Garden Center door. Devon was walking behind me and all I heard was, "ma'am stop." I turn around, see this Mexican dude with his arm wrapped around Devon's throat dragging her back into the store. I immediately sprang into action. I honestly did not know that she had picked up a pack of batteries and I thought this Mexican dude was raping her at said big box store. I mean really, I'm just being honest here. Who in the hell hires Mexican loss prevention officers anyway? And they had nothng on them that notified a person that they were loss prevention. All I saw was this Mexican dude trying to drag my old lady away. I took one step when I was blindsided by another Mexican, the other loss prevention officer. He's telling me to backup, backup and let him do his job. At this point, Devon is screaming bloody murder. I grab this dude by the shirt and sling him into the flowers and potted plants and start marching my way towards Devon and her attacker. At this time I was stopped by a 300 pound mountain of a man, who as it turns out, was the store manager. He put me on my ass and held me there. From here on out things got a little chaotic. They called the law. I called 911 for an ambulance.

Once they found out she had just had brain surgery a year before this and that I had called 911 to report an attack, she was given a citation and told to report to court. We left and went directly to the hospital across the road because my wheels were already spinning. Before we got out of the car I had the "strong arm of the law," John Foy on the phone and had already retained his services. A week later, after reviewing the security camera footage, an entire team of lawyers showed up at our house with smiles on their faces. This is one of the worst attacks they had ever seen in their careers, they said. You can see the dollar signs in their eyes. You can see the dollar signs in our eyes! You could also see the meth in our eyes.

I could probably stop right here with this story and anyone with a lick of common sense could tell you how it ended but I'll go ahead and finish the story

We were set up with doctors and chiropractors by our team of lawyers. We're supposed to go 4 days a week for rehabilitation to our battered bodies, injuries we had suffered at the hands of the evil corporation and their employees. The more we thought about the millions of dollars coming our way, the more dope we did. We missed one appointment. And then another, then an entire week's worth of appointments until finally the law firm dropped us. We were too messed up on meth to go to the chiropractor and doctor visits.

Bye, bye millions of dollars. Thanks, Meth.

Our lives have been interesting, to say the least. Exciting. Sad. Trying. Full of adventure.

I cannot say that we haven't enjoyed it, but it sure would have been nice to hit the litigation Lotto. The quickest way to get rich in America nowadays; sue somebody. But the truth, with that much money I wouldn't be writing this book. I would be in the ground.

No, that wasn't our worldwide fame. Far from it. All the things that we had went through up to this point was a cakewalk compared to what the future held for us.

We got busted.

We were set up by a guy that was also in the dope game. He got myself and three other people. Basically he was taking the competition out. He got popped and his girlfriend was still in jail, so this was his way of getting her out, plus working off the charges he faced.

They came in 17 men deep on us. They blew our French door completely off the hinges and it landed 12 feet away, inside our living room, on our couch. They threw one percussion grenade outside of the house and one inside the house. We were held at gunpoint with automatic weapons for an hour.

They took everything in our house that wasn't bolted down. I was charged with possession of meth with intent to distribute. Devon was charged with forgery for making false IDs.

They tried to get us to cooperate with them and set someone else up by telling us the story of how we got set up. We laughed in their face.

I don't know why I'm thinking about this but you know what, I really dislike SCOOTERS. You can't trust A SCOOTER. Is it a motorcycle or moped? If I ever get money like RICHIE rich, I might buy me a scooter just to find out.

I had welcomed meth back into our home as a guest to help fight boredom and the loneliness that seemed to loom over our relationship, and once again, in the black of night, it had betrayed me.

I remember as I lie face down in our bedroom floor, with a cop's boot cracking two of my ribs, his A-R 15 pointed at my head, that I was finally going to get some rest. That makes me sick to think back on that, and to know there came a point in my life where I felt like I had to go to jail to get some rest.

We had our first appearance 3 days later. The women were on one side of the courtroom and us men were on the other side. It came Devon's turn and the judge started going back and forth, talking about this and that. It sounded like he wasn't going to give her a bond, so I stood up the courtroom and I said, "Your Honor, the only thing that woman is guilty of is having bad taste in men." The entire courtroom broke out in laughter including the judge. He immediately gave her a bond and told me to sit back down and be quiet. I was denied bond. I spent 31 days in county jail before they finally set me a bond and released me.

I got out and went right back to business. Six months later, I'm pulling up to my best friend's house, the same one who bonded me out of Stephens County Jail. I get out of my truck and go knock on his door, and who answers?

The drug task force.

I walked right into the middle of them raiding his house. Or so I thought. Or so I thought.

It's a sad fact, yet still a fact that when people get in trouble, they will FLIP on you in a heartbeat. The HUNTER becomes the hunted. They were there waiting on me.

I was sitting in his living room while they searched my truck. They found $25 worth of dope.

"Well, Alton," begins the drug agent, "seems like we got you now."

"Okay, go ahead and take me to jail, just like you did the last time."

"Well, hold on a minute. You haven't went to court yet on the first charges and now you have these charges and you're being quite uncooperative with us." he continued, "So let me tell you what I'm going to do. If you don't help us this time, I'm going to talk to the DA and I'm going to make sure that you get 40 years."

That got my attention.

"On top of that, think abut this. Both times we got you, you were set up by people that you know well and they weren't the first ones that we sent after you."

That really got my attention.

"And finally, we're going to your house, where we know you keep your supply and that Devon is at home right now waiting on you to get back. We go in there and find what we're looking for and she's at home alone, well, let me just tell you this; you won't be the only one getting 40 years."

"What do you have to say about that?"

"When do you want me to start."

"Thought that one would get you," he said, laughing in my face.

They followed me home, and true to their word made sure they involved Devon and my long time friend who was there, John. They were nice enough to leave the dope alone. Yep. they gave us a list of names they wanted to bust.

We didn't know a single one of them. They were younger than us and loud about their business. The very kind of people that I made it a point to stay away from.

I ain't "da man." Don't want to be "da man." Don't want to know "da man." Don't want to be around anybody who thinks they are "da man." This is all public record, so here goes.

Two days later, they came and said give us someone tonight or kiss your lives goodbye. We met them behind Walmart in Cornelia and I signed up to become a confidential informant. Me, and ONLY ME. NOT DEVON, NOT JOHN.

We had no idea what we were going to do. WE DIDN'T KNOW ANY OF THE PEOPLE THEY WANTED, and we were not about to turn on our friends.

And so we rode around doing dope, trying to figure out our next move. We had put a few feelers out but wasn't getting anything back, when out of the blue, John's phone range.

"Your're never going to believe who that was," John said.

"Who?"

"That was one of the guys from the list. I'd ask someone abut him and they in turn told him that I might be interested in going to work for him."

And so we headed towards his house. We got there and Devon and I stayed in the truck while John got out to go meet the guy in the yard. They spoke for maybe five minutes and John returned to the truck with $40 worth of dope he had purchased, and we drove off.

This guy called us. We didn't call him. We didn't even know him.

Who in the heck sells dope to people that you don't even know, and on top of that, you want them to go to work for you moving your dope because you know, by reputation, they are heavy movers and then they come to you and only buy $40 worth of dope.

The next morning we were in Atlanta when my friend Wanda texted me and asked me if we had heard the news. We didn't have a clue what she was talking about so we Googled the link she sent us and the headlines read, "drug task force throws concussion grenade into baby crib."

The baby boo-boo case. Worldwide headlines. We were questioned by the GBI, the FBI, and US Attorney General's office from Washington DC.

Our lives were now entering the lowest chambers of hell. The local drug task force was "pressuring" us to make sure our story matched their story. It didn't. We had the FBI interrogating us for hours on several different occasions. And we had the US Attorney

General's office demanding we testify in federal court against one of the officers.

Actually they made sure that we testified. Devon was still locked up at PDC when the trial came up, so they had her. The FBI sent the GBI drug unit to my house to pick John up, to hold him in protective custody so he wouldn't run. Which is exactly what we had planned for the next week.

The next day after picking John up, the FBI showed up at my house and for no other reason than just to let me know that the only reason I wasn't in protective custody was the chicken houses. Apparently Devon and John both told them that I was not a flight risk. I wouldn't leave my parents.

And so, the nice FBI lady ended our conversation with, "I'm sure I won't have to come looking for you when it's court day, but I promise you, if I do, I will bury you when I find you."

One good thing did come out of all this thought, at least for us it was good. Due to the police corruption, the charges were dropped, along with six other people, in different cases. The judge who signed the warrants "retired." The chief of police "retired." One officer was fired. The local drug task force was disbanded. No knock warrants are no longer issued in Habersham County. You would have thought that we would have quit while we were ahead. Not us. We just doubled down and expanded our little meth empire.

I had allowed dope to creep back into our lives and now, two years after that first sack, we were ready for the big time. We had hooked up with some folks in Atlanta, who turned out to be some serious players. We were no longer just buying dope, we were transporting pounds of dope and selling guns to the Russian mafia.

Again, no I'm not kidding.

But just to make this clear, I don't know any Russians. Don't want to know any Russians. Cannot, do not, will not be able to identify any Russians. Meth has ruined my memory.

We were sitting in a motel in Gwinnett County with a supplier, who was waiting on the rest of her money to get there. She just got off the phone with her number 1 salesman who said he would be there in 5 minutes with the $12,000 he still owed her. Five minutes later there was a knock at the door.

It was not her number 1 salesman. It was the GBI. I'm just going to give you the bullet points. There were no drugs in the motel room, so no charges. We were told to leave. Two weeks later she shows up at our house with a truckload of meth, followed by the DEA. Yes the federal DEA. She was arrested. As it turns out she was a great record keeper. She really enjoyed writing people's names down and all their drug information.

We were hit the next week, along with 10 other people, with RICO indictments.

A year later Devon's court date came up. I told her lawyer to do whatever he had to do to get her probation. I told him to tell the DA that she was abused by me, scared of me, that I made her do it. Basically put it all on me. And he did.

He called and said that they had come to a plea agreement at the DA's office. We went to court that morning and she got 12 years probation with no prison time. We had a party planned for that night in celebration of Devon coming home without prison, only on probation.

For the first time in our 14-year relationship I was going to smoke a joint with Devon at the party because that's what she wanted.

We walked out of the courtroom, holding hands and feeling more in love than we had in a very long time.

I felt like fate had finally taken a turn and was no longer my enemy, but rather my long lost friend standing by my side once again.

But as you know by now, there's no limit on the lessons I've learned from the School of Hard Knocks.

"Mrs. Fry, I need to speak with you for a moment," said one of the officers that was manning the x-ray machines at the front door. We walked over to the hallway where Devon was immediately handcuffed by a female officer.

"Mrs. Fry, you're under arrest for probation violation of Stephens County," she said.

I couldn't believe what I was hearing. I was so angry I could have chewed rocks. Devon was literally torn out of my arms and whisked away.

Her probation officer out of Stephens County waited until the day that Devon pled guilty to issue a warrant for probation violation.

Mean people suck.

She was crying my name, both our hearts breaking. I moved forward towards her but was restrained by another officer. I was a lunatic lost in grief. We had just jumped one hurdle in our lives only to be smacked in the face with another

I felt both an urgent need to flee before the other shoe dropped, and the desire to stay until the hidden cameras came out to reveal that it was all just a cruel joke.

I stood there in a cold sweat as I glanced at Devon for the last time. I found myself wanting to scream. I felt acid in my throat. My anger was creating this sound, an animalistic growl that I wasn't sure I could contain.

I drove home 90 miles an hour, my ears ringing from the sound of Devon's pleas for help.

Her probation violation was for the RICO charge. Her probation officer was out for blood. She got it.

Six months in Stephens County Jail and then a hundred twenty days in women's PDC, in Claxton Georgia, Four hours away from our home.

I was there an hour early to pick her up on her release date. She was the second one out the door. My God, she felt good in my arms. We looked like we had just robbed a bank as we ran across the parking lot.

They say you can never go home, but we were on our way. The girl of my dreams. My beautiful wife. My best friend.

Six months later, we were divorced.

chapter 76

The Axe Forgets, but the Tree Remembers

Time tends to make people go astray. Your path becomes rutted, a little rougher to travel than you had planned, taking more effort than you thought it should, and before you know it, you're looking for the easy way, a little smoother road to take.

Once again, my life turned to a relentless, agonizing battle with an enemy I could not defeat.

Devon's Revenge.

I'll never forget the afternoon I found out that she was having an affair with my so-called best friend. I felt as though my world just went through an apocalypse. It seemed as if my soul was being ripped into pieces as I watched her pack her belongings and leave for his home, or rather I should say, his Mama's home.

Yes, you should be able to taste the bitterness in that sentence.

There's been times in my life that I thought of myself broken beyond repair. I've had tremendous disappointment that left me both dissatisfied and feeling helpless.

But nothing prepared me for this. My life just became a wasteland, full of debris and rubble. I could not hide from the light of the truth of what had happened and it burnt at my every fiber.

Life had been giving us what we needed to live; love, happiness, a purpose for being. It was beautiful, in its own way. In our way. But it was all a lie.

I began asking myself, was this hardship being imposed on me by God? My just compensation?

A statement that desperately needed delivering?

A statement so thick with humility that I knew whatever my intentions in this matter may be, God was going to insist otherwise.

I prostituted myself to the world, and my obedience was to meth. And now I was learning the hard way that revenge is a dish best served cold.

As if finding out that your wife of 14 years was sleeping with another man, how about this; they were only living 3 miles down the road from our house. That's a little more than any human being should have to take.

My hatred for the both of them became so intense and white hot that I was sure I would burst into flames. My hate was pure black. A beautiful vision where I strip the world of all wrongs, with such energy and force that it became my personal Killing Fields.

I would never starve as long as I have my anger to feed me. Everyday I cluttered my mind with plans and schemes on how I could win Devon back. And if I couldn't win her back? Well...it became a cancer eating away at my soul. The only cure, I told myself, was to destroy the one I had allowed to infect me.

"He" must die.

Luckily for him, he kicked Devon to the curb after she could no longer afford to keep him up in dope. I don't guess the other two or three women kept on rotation really helped the matter either.

And just where did she land, you ask? At none other than my old friend's house. The one who came to get me out of jail in Stephens

County. The one who stole the garbage bag out of the Federal Detention Center with me.

Oh yeah, I forgot, also the one who helped set me up when he got in trouble.

He and I had a few words. Warrants were issued. Excuse me, a warrant was issued.

So the next week Devon and I had a mediation meeting for her divorce. I picked the cheapest mediator I could find, who happened to be an attorney in White County. We met at the courthouse, hashed out our divorce agreement and I made it to the front door.

"Mr. Fry, can I speak with you for a minute?" asked the officer manning the front door x-ray machines.

Deja vu.

"We have a warrant for your arrest out of Habersham County, for battery."

Devon's final twist of the knife was to notify them to look for warrants on me.

The same courthouse, the same scenario, as two years earlier, when Devon had been ripped out of my arms being arrested.

"It's okay purdygurl, love forgives."

Three days later my cell door opened at Habersham County jail and an officer I didn't know walks in.

"Alton Fry?"

"Yes sir?"

"Son, I really hate to do this because I can see you're already having a hard time, but as of two hours ago, you are legally divorced and I'm here to serve you your final decree."

I felt my insides explode and liquefy. I knew it was going to happen, but to be sitting alone, in a jail cell and have it happen was too much.

I had robbed myself of being me. I had allowed madness in my heart and my mind was no longer mine. I had been dying, killing myself, inch by inch, everyone watching, trying to stop me.

BUT I COULDN'T BE STOPPED.

I had been in beast mode.

And now I lay crumpled, like a piece of used paper, in a cold jail cell, sobbing and crying uncontrollably, like an infant who has lost their bottle. Alone.

My God, why can't I just die. Why in the hell are you keeping me alive. My heart is broke, my mind is broke, my soul is void of all feelings. What good am I to you, God? ANSWER ME, DAMMIT! WHAT DO YOU WANT FROM ME?

Blood screamed out to me from the concrete, my little corner of the earth had just collapsed down on me. This was the moment something inside me snapped. I broke.

It's times like these you find out who you really are. And who did I find out I was? Not the smart, anything you want to do man my Dad told me I was. Not the best business partner he ever had, as he always told people. NO, to put it simply; I found out I was a Man on Fire, hell-bent on Revenge. I gathered up my anger and heartache, sharpened them like a two-edged sword and prepared myself to go "All In."

chapter 77

Happy Easter

I felt like the sun had finally went down on me,that I had finally, after all my battles with the world met the end of me.

My mind raced with memories, plans, schemes, and plots, all centered around regaining everything that life had taken from me. It was hard to hear anything or anyone for all the thoughts that rushed through my head on a constant basis. It was like the whitewater of a flooding river; unstoppable, untamable.

And then Devon came home, and then left again, then she came back again, and then she left again. The sad, sick part is that I was choosing to live like this. The first time she came back lasted two days. Then she took off again, after she stole a pack of needles for her newest boyfriend.

Want to know what the real slap in the face was? You're going to love this. It was the same guy that two years earlier had set us up and gotten our doors blown off the hinges by the drug task force.

I began to go through a great Awakening. Every day that went by brought me closer to the truth. I was no longer loved by Devon. As I began to remove the blinders from my eyes, I became able to understand things that had eluded me. I learned it's almost

220

impossible for you mind to overcome your heart. I learned that no one can serve two masters. I had to choose; God or meth. I CHOSE WRONG. I also learned the hardest lesson in my life, sometimes in life, you lose.

It was Easter Sunday. Devon and I had spent the night together at our house, or, I guess now, it was just my house. I spent the night with a mixture of fear and confusion. I feared the same thing happening again; Devon just staying for a day or two and then running off again. I was also in a state of confusion not even really sure what was going on between us. The lines of reality blurred with my emotional exhaustion. I have fleeting moments, memories of the way things once were. But are my memories the truth? Is that the way it was, or just the way I wanted to remember it?

Didn't I ship all the supposed good memories and thoughts away? Replacing them with all the pain that had taken their place? Weren't they supposed to be hidden in the recesses of my troubled mind? Why are they back? What purpose is achieved to explore the bubbling cauldron of my mind, just to tease myself with things I know won't last.

How can a person believe and doubt at the same time, in the same thing? Or rather, should I say, in the same person? All I wanted was to be loved, to have someone that was willing to reach out for me sometime. I was tired of being the fourth man in an three-man race. My life was empty. I was lonely. I was willing to believe anything she said, and cherish every moment of time she was willing to give me. Why, you ask? You already know why. I loved her and I will till the day I die. I worked to hard and too long to let our story end this way. This was not the ending God had planned for our lives. But, of course, Devon had other plans. She left, once again, on Easter morning. The more I sat there the more my mind began to occupy itself with plans of revenge.

Let me tell you something I learned. Revenge is like going out on a limb and then turning around to start sawing off the limb your sitting on. I had given up on life while I was still alive.

With Devon by my side, I felt powerful enough to face down dragons. Without her in my life I felt no more of a man than a blade of grass does.

I had a sickening sensation that started as nothing more than a hunch nestled in the back of my mind which soon bloomed into a revelation of truth.

It was time for the end. EITHER "HIS" OR MINE, I DIDN'T CARE WHICH ONE.

chapter 78

What will I Gain from My Losses

My demons had become like a hurricane that was forming in the sea; everyday getting stronger, just waiting for the perfect moment to strike. And that moment had just arrived. I was about to cloud up and rain all over their parade.

On the day I should have been celebrating Jesus' resurrection, I was, instead driving to "his" house, with no future in sight.

When the fight was over, it looked like this. Devon standing over me screaming at me to get off him because she loved him. Whatever little bit of life, love, manhood, humanity I had left in me disappeared at that very moment. Those words brought me to a standstill. I walked away with nothing left to live for.

My driver's side window had been shattered with a piece of metal. A four inch drain line made of PVC pipe was thrown like a spear through my front window. The rear bumper of Devon's car was now in the back seat. I reckon it's about time for me to head on back to the house.

I'm at the chicken houses as the first one arrives. He left about five minutes of waiting for me to show up. After he leaves, I went back up to the house and decide to call Devon. An hour later they came back, this time with two state patrolmen, two county cars and one county SUV with the drug dogs. By the end of the day I'm in jail for DUI refusal, reckless driving, aggressive driving, leaving the scene of an accident and the biggie...Aggravated assault. And whose name was on the police statement against me?

It's okay, love forgives.

Never mind that it was lies. They had me. Never mind the fact that a month later Devon went to my attorneys in both Habersham (my new charges) and White County (my probation charges because of the new charge) and told them both that she was forced to sign a false statement. It didn't matter, it was way too late.

So now you know why I'm here. Locked up in Carlton H Colwell Probation Detention Center in Blairsville, Georgia writing this book.

On mine and Devon's way home two years ago when she was released from Claxton PDC, we had a very serious conversation and I told her these very words.

"You'll never be happy or satisfied until I go to prison, will you? That way we're even," I asked her. Honest to God. It's okay though, love doesn't keep score. Love doesn't hurt, it forgives. I love you, Devon.

chapter 79

The Last Saturday 2-13-18

This is my last Saturday at Colwell PDC. I have sat here on my bed for the last 175 days, allowing the crushing weight to my stupidity to try and destroy what dreams I have left.

You have no privacy here at Colwell. Even my dreams, my fantasies are hard to hide in this madness. I try to flee my body, to escape my distress and pain. It doesn't work. I always come back to the pain and wind up feeling like a Jack In The Box. Ready to pop at any moment. I did however, catch myself in a happy moment tonight. I got a letter from Wanda telling me she would be here Friday to pick me up and that her and Devon have been making plans for my Great Escape. Yes, even after all I have endured my heart still lies with Devon. I know, I know, I'm living on the far side of common sense.

Some days I have difficulty even remembering what Devon looks like. I have forgotten her laugh, her smile. But I have no doubt that come Friday morning when I walk out of here and see her I will know her. When our fingers touch and our hands embrace we will relive 16 years of love in just a second. When our lips collide in a tender symphony of passion it will ignite every memory of a love that was meant to be.

I know I still have a long way to go before my spirit is able to smile again. Before I'm totally able to relax in life. Even with a survivor's heart, this tent of anger that I sometimes find myself living in tends to take me down an aimless and lonely road. It's the path that I have traveled many times in my life before. Always leaving me with a sense of frustration and suffocating from life's pressures.

But not this time. The last ten months have been a life lesson sent by God. I WILL NOT be swallowed up by life again. There are no other answers I seek in the night. No matter how long or how laborious life becomes I cannot, I will not, allow myself to be devoured again by the trappings of the world. I simply cannot.

Meiji

It was well after Easter. I knew what was going to happen, I just didn't know when or where. I just finished up at the chicken houses and decided to drive the tractor back up to the house to do some yard work. I turned into the driveway and was immediately facing a Habersham County Sheriff's department patrol car with two deputies in it. I had nowhere to go. I couldn't outrun them. My tractor is nice, but it only has a top speed of 17 miles per house. I had a brief, but very surreal vision, of using the front bucket and scooping the patrol car up and dropping it off the bank. Nah, better not.

"What can I do for you fellows?"

"We have a warrant for your arrest our of White County for probation violation," the officer said, knowing that I already knew what the answer was. And so I went to jail, smelling like a chicken and in desperate need of a shot of dope. They wouldn't even let me take my chicken house boots off and go get some shoes and put on. They cuffed and stuffed me and we were gone in a flash.

They say there's two types of people in the world; ones who watch the news and ones who make the news. You can guess which one I am. Good news was that the "Sunday Easter chaos" didn't make the front page. The bad news is that it took up over half the entire second page. At least that's what my poor Mom told me on her first visit to see me at the White County Jail.

I learned a lot of things the four months I was locked up there in White County. The first thing I learned was that I, in no way, shape, or form, enjoyed doing time. I also learned that I had been ignoring the things in life that had really mattered. The kind of things my Dad taught me about. No matter how much my mind tries to wring out my past, it will never be enough to clean it. Nor should it. I want it to stand as a testament to where I've been and just how far I've come. I also learned about humility and forgiveness while being locked up. I've learned to swallow my pride, what little I had left and my understanding and patience of other people has reached heavenly heights. But I guess my most important lesson has also been my greatest gift; I learned to walk with God, NOT AGAIN, but truly for the first time in my life.

I was too stupid to understand the destruction I've been doing to myself. I had allowed hate and jealousy to cloud my mind to the point that I now found myself facing 20 years in prison. I felt that I was so far gone that I could never find my way back home. That was when I started collecting those pills in White County Jail to kill myself, but as you already know, God had other plans for me.

I guess that old saying is true, "if you want to hear God laugh, just tell him your plans."

I am now at peace. Not only with myself, but with the world. Yes, I'm nervous, maybe a little scared, but I'm also full of hope once again. Hope for a future, hope for love and hope to just be little Alton once again.

chapter 81

The End

Today is the day. I'm going home in just a few minutes. It's been 290 days since the last time I've seen home. Later, when I look back on this section of my life story it will be nothing more than a bad dream I had. My body and soul will be as one. My heart and soul will once again be in unison.

The feelings that pulse through me no longer scare me. They now lift me up with excitement of life.

My writing has become my only friend. With God's blessings I have allowed it to take control of my life. More than anything, it has helped me to heal this jagged wound left by my final battle with meth, one that I almost lost.

But God reassured me I would once again see brighter days, more glorious than I've ever dreamed. I can see them on the horizon. PRAISE GOD, PRAISE GOD. I have now learned to shut out the phantom voices in my head and listen to God.

It's tough, though, because sometimes I don't really like what God has to say. He makes me mad with all the sense he makes. I no longer dream of revenge or acts of terror. Nor of money or power. I now dream a more simple dream. Freedom. Freedom for both my body and my mind. Free to enjoy the peace and love that I know awaits me. Free from the nightmare meth. That darkness that I once embraced as my lover now only offends me. Like Custer, I made my last stand, only I was blessed enough to have God walk me out of my Badlands.

"Detainee Fry," booms over the loudspeaker. "Gather all of you state belongings and report to central control."

That's me. That is me they're talking to. Dear God, I'm finding it hard to move, my eyes are full of tears. I'm going home. I get to kiss Devon. I get to take my Mom shopping. I get to take care of my Dad. I get to be a man again. I get to ask Taylor if she will forgive me, and maybe, just maybe, if I'm lucky we can be Daddy and daughter again. I promise all of you I'm going to make you proud.

It is at this moment, with a half-hearted smile, I realize that I am finally ready for NORMAL PEOPLES PROBLEMS.

"Here's your street clothes, Fry. Step into the laundry and change and you'll be free to go."

"Thank you, sir."

I make it through the security doors without anyone stopping me. I make it to the front door, where the sergeant on duty is standing.

"Good luck, Fry," he says.

"Is that it, sir?"

"That's it. You're a free man. Don't come back."

"I don't plan on it," I reply as I walk out the front doors.

God is everywhere. I now realize that. I take a few minutes to gaze at the sun. My God, the silence. I can hear myself breathing. My heart is pounding in my chest. My mind is exploding from all the senses that surround me. I raise my hand to shield my weary eyes from that beautiful glow that I have been deprived of for the last four months. I AM CLAD IN PERFECT HAPPINESS.

And there she is, at the other end of the parking lot. Standing and waiting on me. I once told myself it would be easier to die in here than it would be to live free. I no longer believe that as I bend to give her a hug and a kiss on the cheek.

"Hey Mom," I whisper through my tears.

"Hello son. I've come to take you home."

CPSIA information can be obtained
at www.ICGtesting.com
Printed in the USA
FFHW022002271118
49676062-54059FF